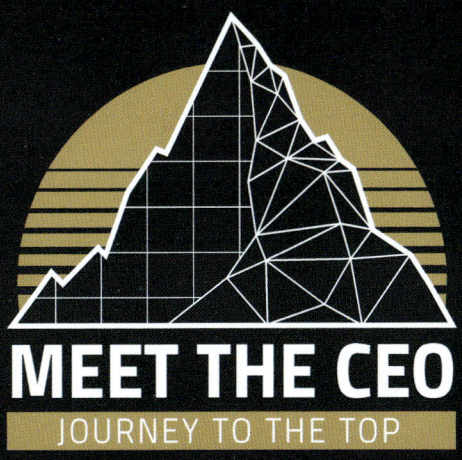

MEET THE CEO

JOURNEY TO THE TOP

TO ....

....

SIGNED ....

SUHAIL MIRZA

RECRUITMENT LEADERS

THEIR JOURNEY TO THE TOP
AND HOW YOU CAN JOIN THEM

SUHAIL MIRZA

RACS Publishing Limited
RACS Group House - Three Horseshoes Walk
Warminster - Wiltshire - BA12 9BT

Published by RACS Publishing Limited 2016
www.racspublishing.com

10 9 8 7 6 5 4 3 2 1

A catalogue record for this book
is available from the British Library

ISBN: 978-1-5272-0005-0

Designed by RACS Marketing Limited
www.racsmarketing.com

Printed & Bound in Great Britain by
CPI ANTONY ROWE

ABOUT THE AUTHOR

Within the recruitment and support services sectors
Suhail Mirza is a very well known and respected figure.

A former solicitor who specialised in employment, he has
been involved in the recruitment, healthcare and support
services business sectors over the past decade or more.

Over the past decade he has partnered investors in the
sector to grow their businesses (organically and through
acquisition). As well as being a non-Executive Director at
RACS Group, he is Chairman of H1 Healthcare. His wider
business interests encompass retail and information
marketing sectors.

Suhail was co-owner of a family healthcare business for
12 years (employing more than 200 people) which was
successfully sold in 2014. He continued his interests in
healthcare with Alium Partners and writing for leading trade
journals including Recruitment International, Caring Times,
Healthcare Market News and Community Care Market News.

PRAISE FOR
MEET THE CEO

"*Meet the CEO* provides an interesting insight to the person behind the face and the journey they have taken, whilst promoting the merits of the sector which is so often maligned".

Richard Herring
Managing Director & Snr Vice President - Volt

"Suhail is very well networked and connected within the recruitment world and he is always able to provide interesting insights into what is going on."

Russell Thompson
Group Managing Director - LMA Recruitment

"Suhail's numerous publications are interesting, insightful and challenge thought, his *Meet the CEO* piece in *Recruitment International* is particularly good."

Lawrence Hargreaves
Director Source Technology &
Former Managing Director - Nicoll Curtin

MEET THE CEO
JOURNEY TO THE TOP

BY SUHAIL MIRZA

I am indebted first and foremost to the 32 leaders who appear in this book and who have been generous in their time in meeting me regularly and sharing - often with refreshing candour - their journeys in recruitment and business in general. That many have become friends whose company is always enriching is a blessing.

David Head and Teri Etherington at *Recruitment International* have been invaluable in their support of the "Meet the CEO" series since its inception in the spring of 2014 and also in helping with key elements in the preparation of the book.

I also wish to acknowledge my debt to three outstanding international business scholars and wonderful teachers.

Professor Stanley K Ridgley at Drexel University's LeBow College of Business: a former military intelligence officer for the US army, his

SPECIAL THANKS

Special mention must be made of my friend and business partner, Terry Hillier, founder and MD at RACS Group. A man of action, Terry (like the leaders in this book) has a gift of turning the possible into reality (at speed!) and without his personal and professional support and partnership this book would have simply remained a wonderful idea.

work on 'strategic thinking skills' has been a source of inspiration and wisdom for much of the thematic organisation of this book. Thank you Professor Stan.

Professor Michael A Roberto from Bryant University (formerly on the faculty at Harvard Business School) has generously permitted me to draw on his work on 'Transformational Leadership' during my research for the book.

Professor Ryan Hamilton of Emory University's Goizueta Business School has illuminated my understanding of marketing and his guidance on the critical distinction between strategic (which must come first) and operational marketing has not only been invaluable for this book but for all my business interests.

It is hoped that the book and the legacy created by the 32 featured leaders demonstrates how they and the sector itself reflect and can contribute to the very best and most up to date thinking from business scholarship around the world.

Finally, I want to thank the many recruitment professionals (CEOs, managers and consultants) who have, over the past few years, so graciously expressed the value they have received from reading the Meet the CEO features published monthly in *Recruitment International*. Their kind and sincere feedback emboldened me to create this book and their support for the idea provided the additional inspiration always needed for undertakings of this nature.

FOREWORD

BY GARY ASHWORTH - FOUNDER AND EXECUTIVE CHAIRMAN
INTERQUEST GROUP PLC

Owning or working in a recruitment company is a precarious business. The rules change very quickly. It's like learning a card game and just when you think you've mastered it, you find that two new cards have been introduced into the deck and you have to adopt a new strategy to win.

Anyone can be lucky once, but some of the people featured in this book are true industry leaders who have learned to overcome a whole host of obstacles and been successful again and again. Many are happy to share their secrets and strategies to let the reader decide the best route to the top.

Like many industries, the selection and recruitment of staff is constantly evolving. We have had to learn to adapt to a growing contingent workforce, disruptive technologies, MSP/RPO providers, headcount freezes, umbrella companies, contract novation, diversity targets, changing legislation and margin erosion as well as liaising with customers with growing 'client side' recruitment competence. Some of the 'easy-to-fill' roles have gone forever.

The CEOs you will meet in this book have demonstrated the leadership and vision to see through the mist and work out how to predict the future, and design a strategy to outpace their competitors.

They've created structures where people thrive too. Recruitment has been described as a cake-eating contest where first prize is more cake!

Yet many of the leaders featured have created a learning environment where there are well-paid consultants and career progression alongside high levels of customer satisfaction and integrity.

Like most industries there are heroes and villains (and some of those reading this book will know who they are!). Certain sectors are cyclical too and profits can be highly geared depending on the growth or decline of the economy, which leads to the investment community remaining cautious of the sector.

Despite all of these challenges, a simple principle remains, which is that *"If you have access to rare communities of talent with in-demand skill-sets, clients will pay handsomely to get them."*

The various trade bodies, publications, conferences and training organisations have done great work to improve the standards of service received by candidates and clients alike and recruitment is now a proper career in its own right. It is a true meritocracy where people can thrive despite background, age or qualification.

The future looks brighter than ever. We have created a culture where people change permanent jobs more often without stigma and many people have chosen a career as professional temps/interims/contractors in all fields spanning consultancy through financial markets, health care and the new digital economy.

Suhail Mirza is himself an expert in his field. A 'trusted source of knowledge' in the industry. He knows the people and the trends across recruitment. As a biographer, he has the uncanny ability to cut through the waffle and focus on the precise issues that separate the winners from the 'also-rans.'

Meet the CEO is a compelling read and an essential handbook for those already involved in the industry or who are interested in pursuing a rewarding career in this exciting business.

PRAISE FOR
MEET THE CEO

"Suhail is an exceptionally knowledgeable and well connected individual within the Recruitment Industry. He is an individual I respect very much and his *Meet the CEO* is required reading."

Darren Ryemill
CEO - Opus Professional Services Group
Entrepreneur of the Year (*Recruitment International Awards* - 2013)

"I have known Suhail for a number of years and his *Meet the CEO* series is excellent reading."

Stuart Britton
CEO - RDL Corporation

"Suhail is extremely well-regarded within the Recruitment Sector and with good reason. He not only has an in-depth knowledge of key verticals, but is arguably one of the best-connected people in the Industry."

Charlie Walker
Entrepreneur of the Year (*Recruitment International Awards* - 2014)

CONTENTS

PART I THE RECRUITMENT SPACE

01

14-19
**WHY THE
STORIES NEED
TO BE TOLD**

02

20-25
**THE WORLD OF
RECRUITMENT**

03

26-31
**THE BUSINESS
OF LEADERSHIP**

06

108-113 **AUDENTES FORTUNA
JUVAT - COURAGE**
114-117 **Toni Cocozza** MD - DP Connect
118-121 **Charlie Walker**
(Former CEO - Vivid Resourcing)
122-125 **Adam Shulman**
CEO - Simply Education
126-131 **David Cook**
MD - National Locums
132-137 **Matthew Eames**
CEO - Eames Consulting
138-141 **Andy Hogarth**
CEO - Staffline

07

142-145 **INFLECTION POINTS - FORTITUDE**
146-149 **Albert Ellis** CEO - Harvey Nash
150-153 **Richard Herring** MD - Volt
154-159 **Michelle Watson**
CEO - Gemini People
160-165 **John Hailstone** CEO - Compello
Staffing Group
166-171 **Karen Silk** CEO - Capital
International Staffing
172-177 **Jason Stewart**
CEO - DRC Locums
178-181 **Steve Ingham**
CEO - PageGroup

PART II LEADERS AND THEIR JOURNEYS

04

34-37	**STRATEGIC INTENT - VISION**
38-41	**Dean Kelly** CEO - Synarbor plc
42-47	**Robert Thesiger** CEO - Fiser Group
48-53	**Jane Lovell** MD - Cooper Lomaz
54-57	**Alan McBride** MD - Camino Partners
58-63	**Julie O'Neill** MD - McCall
64-69	**Darren Ryemill** CEO - Opus Professional Services Group

05

70-73	**COUP D'OEIL - INTUITION**
74-79	**Sue Cooper** CEO - Morgan Hunt
80-83	**Scott Bulloch** MD - ATA Recruitment
84-89	**Mike Gawthorne** CEO - Serocor
90-95	**Stuart Britton** CEO - RDL Corporation
96-99	**Paul Jameson** MD - Outsource UK
100-103	**Greg Latham** MD - Encore Personnel
104-107	**Pam Easen** CEO - H1 Healthcare

PART III THE FUTURE IS HAPPENING NOW

08

182-185	**BLUE OCEANS IMAGINATION**
186-189	**Gary Ashworth** Chairman Interquest Group plc
190-195	**Adam Buck** CEO Phaidon International
196-199	**Andrea Williams** MD - Ambition
200-203	**David Rai** CEO - Testing Circle
204-207	**Andrew Larholt** CEO - Montash
208-213	**Joost Kreulen** CEO Empresaria Group plc

09

216-221	**LESSONS FROM THE LEADERS**

10

222-227	**THE FUTURE OF RECRUITMENT IS HERE NOW**

PART ONE

THE RECRUITMENT SPACE

CHAPTERS

01
14-19
WHY THE STORIES NEED TO BE TOLD

02
20-25
THE WORLD OF RECRUITMENT

03
26-31
THE BUSINESS OF LEADERSHIP

01

WHY THE STORIES NEEDED TO BE TOLD

A Thriving Industry

The Recruitment Sector is thriving. It matters and plays a critical role in the UK economy (and indeed globally). According to *Recruitment International* in 2014/15 the recruitment industry turned over £31.5 billion and employs more than 100,000 people. Many recruitment businesses appear in the Sunday Times Best Companies to Work For awards each year.

Finding a permanent job has been revealed in some surveys as the most important life decision people have to make. In addition, having a flexible pool of talent, to undertake temporary and contract projects, is seen as mission critical for UK industry as it competes in a globalised workplace.

THIS IS THE BEST TIME SINCE THE 1980S TO BE RUNNING A RECRUITMENT BUSINESS..."

Furthermore the labour market is undergoing profound transformation.

Whilst this brings deep challenges to the current recruitment business models, the widely recognised 'skills shortage' should offer great opportunities too.

Little wonder then that Kevin Greene, the CEO of the Recruitment and Employment Confederation (REC), was moved to comment in March 2016:

"This the best time since the 1980s to be running a recruitment business" and went on to *"forecast growth of 22% for the industry in the next two and half years."*

A Tarnished Reputation

Despite all of the above the sector's reputation with both candidates and clients (and perhaps even amongst those that have or currently work within it) remains decidedly mixed. *Recruiter Magazine*, in January 2014, described the industry's reputation as 'damaged.'

This was affirmed in October 2015 by Nick Bowles, Head of Stakeholder Engagement at APSCo (The Association of Professional Staffing Companies), who was moved to assert: *"the reputation of the recruitment sector is often seen as quite tarnished."*

The negative perceptions include accusations of the 'immoral use' of fake online job ads to attract graduates to hand over CVs and ⟩

(according to a 2011 survey conducted by APSCo and Recruitment Solutions Group) candidates criticising agencies for being primarily motivated by financial rewards.

That survey also highlighted that clients expect more from agencies in terms of being transparent and having a better understanding of their business.

Perhaps as worryingly, concerns about the sector emanate from those working within it. According to REC research from July 2015 nearly a quarter of recruitment consultants are dissatisfied with their pay and rewards. And the APSCo Deloitte Recruitment Index 2015 reveals concerning churn rates within recruitment businesses with even the largest ones reporting between 24% and 36% of staff leaving within less than 12 months.

There has been a range of initiatives from the likes of REC and APSCo to address this reputation issue.

The REC on 28th June 2016 issued a 'toolkit' designed to help recruiters raise the profile of their businesses and to help *"improve the reputation of the industry as a whole"*.

In a similar vein Ann Swain, CEO at APSCo, the trade body which has represented those in the recruitment of professional talent since 1999, has been strident in her calls to ensure all efforts are made to improve the reputation of the sector and has led calls for creating a new universal standard for the sector as a whole to achieve this.

CLIENTS EXPECT MORE FROM AGENCIES IN TERMS OF BEING TRANSPARENT AND HAVING A BETTER UNDERSTANDING OF THEIR BUSINESS."

And Kevin Greene's 'rallying cry', in September 2015, to be proactive to promote the positive impact of the sector under the general strap line "Jobs Transform Lives" is something all who care about the sector should stand behind.

And yet in 2015 we saw the sector continued to be maligned from those at the very top of public life.

Most notable perhaps has been the Health Secretary, Jeremy Hunt, last year accusing recruiters of *"ripping off the NHS"* alongside the National Union of Teachers seeking to lobby against the very presence of recruitment agencies in the education sector. Both attacks take little account of the profoundly important value recruiters bring to each of these sectors and the role they play in making sure patients and children respectively receive the services they need in a safe, timely and professional manner.

Time for Pride: From Those Who Know

Having known so many leaders within recruitment for many years the disconnect between these attacks and negative perceptions and the reality of what these leaders had achieved and their commitment to setting the highest standards of professionalism within the sector was deeply concerning. Especially as one of the leading current concerns for all recruiters is attracting new talent to work within the sector. ⟩

Accordingly, approximately two years ago I sat with a broad group of CEOs of leading recruitment businesses ranging from stock exchange listed companies to thriving privately held SMEs operating across a wide range of sectors, to see how we could help highlight some of the unique attractions of the sector as well as the pivotal importance it plays in the economy.

What became obvious was that one of the least well known aspects of the recruitment sector was the sheer depth and breadth of talent that leads it. The stories of such leaders were virtually unknown to anyone outside their respective businesses. And yet the stories whenever shared have proved compelling to recruiters and those outside the sector.

This is hardly surprising, the leaders featured here range from Oxford graduates to those who left school at 16 with few or no qualifications. It features those who began their businesses in their twenties to those who entered recruitment as a second or even third career. Some have worked through several recessions while others set up their business in the aftermath of the last one!

And the journeys (including trials and triumphs) these leaders have undertaken along the way, it was agreed, put paid to some of the myths created about the sector particularly from those who should be better informed.

And thus the 'Meet the CEO' article series in *Recruitment International* was born in the spring of 2014.

SURVEY AFTER SURVEY REVEALS THAT AN 'INSPIRING VISION' IS A KEY DRIVER OF ENGAGING WITH TODAY'S JOBSEEKERS."

I have been humbled by the wonderful feedback that the series has generated from across the recruitment sector and beyond. Recruitment consultants have found that the CEO stories offered them a glimpse of the experience of this disparate group of leaders and has inspired them in their careers. CEOs from across the sector have said that it has been deeply informative to learn about how their peers have reached the top.

And equally importantly, as the sector seeks to attract talent from outside the industry, we have received many comments from those working in different sectors (as well as those soon to complete their formal education) stating they now viewed the recruitment sector as one they should investigate further as a career choice.

Survey after survey reveals that an 'inspiring vision' is a key driver of engagement with today's jobseekers. CIETT (the body created to promote the common interests of the recruitment sector globally) highlights that pride, hope and trust are key, value-adding elements that recruiters bring to the world of work.

It was for these reasons that I wrote the book and whilst it draws on the best business school scholarship, it is not meant to be a 'how to' manual but rather a meditation on the 'why' recruitment, I believe that the richest insights into this question come from the journeys and wisdom of the leaders themselves.

02

THE WORLD OF
RECRUITMENT

If you work in recruitment (or are thinking about doing so) there are plenty of reasons to be proud about it.

Staggering Statistics

Yet the recruitment sector may be the best kept secret in the world of business and/or the least understood or appreciated as we alluded to in the opening chapter given its continued, very mixed reputation.

I say 'best kept secret' because just a glance at the facts and figures in respect of the sector - especially for those not familiar with it - is highly instructive:

Taking the UK alone, based on the REC/HSBC 'Recruitment Industry Trends Survey 2014/15':

▲ Total industry turnover reached £31.5 billion in 2014/15, an increase of 9.7% from the previous year
▲ The industry helped place 634,000 people into permanent work in 2014/15
▲ Some 1.2 million on any given day during 2014/15 were undertaking temp, contract or interim assignments facilitated by a recruiter
▲ The total number of people working in the sector stands at 103,000

THIS IS THE BEST TIME SINCE THE 1980S TO BE RUNNING A RECRUITMENT BUSINESS..."

This is a story of growth and recovery. The industry was turning over £3 billion in 1993 so is now ten times bigger. It has also bounced back since the global financial crisis began in 2007/08 growing 16.5% since that time.

It is, however possible that the above numbers may underestimate the total turnover value for the UK recruitment sector. According to *Recruitment International's* TOP 500 Report 2016 it estimates that total turnover could be closer to £40 billion and that the numbers of recruitment agencies are increasing with RI estimating 8,000 operating in 2015.

And the professionalism of the sector continues apace with significant work being undertaken by the likes of the REC and APSCo, both prominent trade bodies representing the interests of the sector.

If we step further back and take a look at the global scale of the sector the numbers become even more eye-watering. Based on the CIETT (International Confederation of Private Employment Services) Economic Report 2016 the global impact of the recruitment sector is profound:

- ▲ An industry turnover of 450 billion euros
- ▲ Employing 1.6 million people within agencies
- ▲ Providing access to the labour market for 71.9 million people
- ▲ Filling over 30 million full time jobs in 2014 〉

The arresting fact is that agency work alone accounted for only 1.6% of the global labour market so the opportunity (particularly as emerging economies develop greater flexibility within their labour markets) remains immense.

But it's Always More Than the Numbers

Global and UK labour markets are unrecognisable from just a couple of decades ago and as CIETT President, Annemarie Muntz says:

"The employment and recruitment industry is helping companies and workers to adapt to the 21st century challenges facing the labour market."

The challenges include digitisation, globalisation, demographic change, skills shortages and new attitudes to the world of work itself.

Returning to the UK and looking at just a few of these challenges we can see how the industry and some of the leaders featured in this book are playing a vital role helping clients and candidates address them.

It is nearly 10 years since Lord Leitch warned *"Prosperity for all in the global economy - world class skills"* - December 2006 that the UK's skills base was not world class and the UK therefore ran the risk of undermining its long term prosperity. It is clear much work still needs to be done to meet the yawning 'skills gap' facing the nation. And recruitment agencies have and continue to play their part in addressing this critical issue.

"THE EMPLOYMENT AND RECRUITMENT INDUSTRY IS HELPING COMPANIES AND WORKERS TO ADAPT TO THE 21ST CENTURY CHALLENGES FACING THE LABOUR MARKET."

Public Sector Services

For example, a recent REC Survey has found almost 90% of agencies in the healthcare, social care, education and local government markers are facing difficulty to fill vacancies. At a time of austerity and given the critically important social role these sectors play recruiters can take pride in the ways many are going the extra mile to help.

In the education sector Dean Kelly (in chapter 4) explains the innovative work undertaken while he was CEO at Synarbor. This included working with a Local Education Authority to engineer the dramatic turnaround in a school's performance taking it out of special measures. And indeed according to a REC survey in 2015 within education, some 80% of education recruitment agencies had persuaded a teacher to remain in the profession rather than leave it; a truly staggering impact that largely goes unnoticed.

Within healthcare the story of how David Cook (chapter 6) and National Locums' commitment to help the Noble hospital on the Isle of Man attract vital staff is inspiring for all the sector as is the very personal drive for David to help the NHS given his young son's need for highly specialised surgery.

And this is not to overlook the rigorous compliance and other checks that recruiters undertake in both education and health to ensure our children and often vulnerable service users are in safe hands. >

Private Sector Skills Shortages

The skills shortage identified by the Leitch Review spanned many sectors but the engineering sector is of particular significance as Government policy recognises the need to 're-balance' the economy, away from an over-reliance on the services sector. Cambridge Economics Professor Ha-Joon Change has eloquently spelled out the dangers of reducing the importance of manufacturing for an economy in his wonderful *23 Things they don't tell you about Capitalism* (2010). Heartening to see at least some experts are being heard!

A number of the leaders featured in this book have extensive experience in the broadly defined engineering recruitment sector and we shall see in chapter 5 how Scott Bulloch and Mike Gawthorne started rail and engineering practices (from scratch) at ATA and ARM (now part of Serocor) respectively.

Diversity

The question of diversity has rightly become of central importance in labour market policy not only as a good in its own right but also due to the economic sense it makes to ensure the world of work is ever more inclusive.

We in the UK have achieved much over the decades since the Equal Pay legislation took effect more than 40 years ago but we have much work still to do. The 2014 Report from the Global Economic Forum, for example, worryingly found that the UK had, for the first time, dropped out of the top 20 gender-equal countries. Iceland was placed number one and clearly being easily bested by that Nordic nation is becoming a regular occurrence!

There are of course many areas of the labour market where the need for more effective diversity is imperative. The ageing nature of the workforce is one example and given the growing number of older people in the UK workforce in the next few years Baroness Altmann CBE (until July 2016 the Pensions Minister) has identified the crucial role recruiters can play to help such workers lead fuller working lives.

In addition to the principled commitments from the likes of REC and APSCo many of our leaders in this book have and continue to play prominent roles to shape and develop the Diversity agenda.

Karen Silk (chapter 7), an eloquent and impassioned champion of the role of women in engineering is a great example, as are Albert Ellis and Harvey Nash's 'Inspire' and 'Engage' initiatives. One could cite many more including Rob Thesiger (chapter 4) and FISER Group's 'City Talent' programme and more than one person has said that Sue Cooper's story (chapter 5) within recruitment is itself a living testament to the values of diversity!

▲ **The Recruitment Sector plays a crucial role in the global labour market**
▲ **Its global turnover stands at 450 billion euros and it employs 1.6 million people**
▲ **In the UK it helped 630,000 people get permanent work in 2014/15**
▲ **More than 100,000 people work in the UK recruitment sector**
▲ **The world of work is changing and recruiters are playing lead roles in many areas to help tackle the skills shortages in the UK as well as promoting the value of diversity.**
▲ **You would be right to be proud to be a recruiter!**

THE BUSINESS
OF LEADERSHIP

Every one of the outstanding recruitment professionals featured in this book are by definition outstanding business leaders; some have only been in the sector a few years while others have been here a few decades!

The words 'business' and 'leadership' are thrown around a lot and are often taken for granted. If we take a moment to understand their meaning properly, we can gain a better insight into the true scale of achievement of all those featured in the next section of the book and be better able to take away the key lessons (whatever the latest fad or business 'management technique' may be) that can be used by any recruiter in his or her career.

Creating Value

We live in an era of fierce competition and nowhere more so than in recruitment. People often define the goal of business as making a profit from its operations. The problem with this is that it is inward looking; focusing on what the company does and receives.

ACCORDING TO BUSINESS WRITER JOAN MAGRETTA YOU IGNORE STRATEGY AT YOUR OWN PERIL."

The most creative business thinking now enjoins us to view the true purpose of business as creating value for its intended customers and accordingly the focus for business decisions should be outward looking. As Professor of Marketing, Ryan Hamilton, advises if we want a truly strategic marketing approach all businesses must first know:

- ▲ Who are my customers?
- ▲ What do they value?
- ▲ How can I deliver this in a differentiated way?

Strategy: Lessons from War

As we shall see differentiation is the foundation of the often used but ill-defined core business concept of Strategy. And make no mistake, strategy matters. According to business writer Joan Magretta, you ignore strategy at your own peril.

The term itself draws heavily from the history of military theorists who were able to arrange resources in a way that allowed their armies to defeat the enemy, sometimes against opponents with seemingly far greater resources. The principles of successful military strategy were codified for modern times in the 19th century and two of the most notable names are Antoine Jomini and Carl Von Clausewitz. The former was an officer in Napoleon's army and is often credited in his *Art of War-1838* with drawing the distinction between strategy, tactics and logistics.〉

Von Clausewitz was a Prussian officer, a contemporary of Jomini (they didn't like each other much!) and his *On War* (1832) is one of the most influential treatises on the subject. He emphasised the role of 'chance' or the unexpected - which business faces everyday! - in conflict and argued that, however elaborate your plan may be, the great leader needs to be able to think on their feet in the face of a fluid reality.

Strategy in Business

Much of the above was enlisted in support of the creation of 'Strategy' as a core subject in Business Schools. And Professor Michael Porter of Harvard is often credited with almost single-handedly creating the new field of business strategy with a series of important books in the 1980s.

He says: *"Competitive strategy is about being different. It means deliberately choosing a different set of activities to deliver a unique mix of value"* in his hugely influential article *What is Strategy?* from the Harvard Business Review 1996.

He of course accepts that 'operational effectiveness' is important but it is not synonymous with strategy; and strategy is not a checklist or simply a grand statement. It means having a clear vision, building a set of choices of how to use your resources to fulfil it and then constantly undertaking change and refining your offering to realise that vision.

And this allows you to capture as much of the value you create for customers as possible. It does not necessarily require you to be the

COMPETITIVE STRATEGY IS ABOUT BEING DIFFERENT. IT MEANS DELIBERATELY CHOOSING A DIFFERENT SET OF ACTIVITIES TO DELIVER A UNIQUE MIX OF VALUE."

best and beat the competition on all fronts; rather it demands that your business be different and stand out from the competition through the unique way you add value to your customers.

This can be based on serving highly specialised niche markets with relatively few other competitors (the stories of Adam Buck, Matthew Eames and Gary Ashworth come to mind) or having a distinct mix of services or markets in which you operate (David Rai, Sue Cooper and Karen Silk's stories are relevant here).

Of equal value is Professor Porter's insight that *"Strategy renders choices about what not to do as important as choices about what to do."*

These principles of a good strategy remain timeless and go to the heart of *why* you are in business at all rather than simply focusing on how you should conduct your business. It is the difference between being *efficient* (doing things right) and being *effective* (doing the right things).

The Value of Leadership

Strategy and vision are foundational but without effective and inspirational leadership they remain just words. >

'Leadership' is also a term that we have chosen deliberately. Sometimes distinctions are drawn between leadership and management, as well as between these two and entrepreneurship. We think this is too narrow and does not fit into the 21st century age of fast start-ups where the ability to create new ventures and lead/manage them immediately are all part of the price the current age requires of its visionaries.

As the refreshingly exciting business book, *The Lean Startup* from Eric Ries argues:

"Entrepreneurship is a kind of management... We lack a coherent management paradigm for new innovative ventures."

With acknowledgement to the work of Joan Magretta (the former Strategy Editor of the Harvard Business Review), we view leadership as the genius of being able to transform complexity and specialisation into performance. In other words, being able to organise people, resources, plans (all within ever-changing market conditions) into the realisation of an agreed vision.

Anyone who has been asked to set up a desk in the world of recruitment is a leader, a manager and entrepreneur all at once! A look at the stories of Steve Ingham and Andrea Williams are testimony to that, as each led the growth of divisions within an already established business in the early part of their careers. Similarly, Sue Cooper and Michelle Watson's experiences of building up distinct businesses within Michael Page are entrepreneurial in its true sense!

Other leaders featured left successful recruitment careers to set up their own businesses and sometimes with many years of business

ENTREPRENEURSHIP IS A KIND OF MANAGEMENT... WE LACK A COHERENT MANAGEMENT PARADIGM FOR NEW INNOVATIVE VENTURES."

experience behind them (see Adam Buck or Andy Larholt) and sometimes with very little recruitment experience! (See Pam Easen, Charlie Walker or Paul Jameson).

Harvard business scholar John Kotter identifies the importance of creating a compelling vision, aligning people to this vision and being able to motivate and inspire people to make the inevitable changes along the way to making that vision a Reality. These are the key components of great leadership, in addition to having the right values to animate this process is fundamental.

In the next section we organise the stories of the 32 leaders into five key categories or principles which business scholarship highlights as indispensable to commercial success. All our featured leaders exude all five principles (and others we list in chapter 9) but these five act as organising concepts which we trust help to better understand the lessons from the leaders' journeys.

Concepts are important but can be abstract. What makes them truly come alive so they become calls to action are the stories of those who have put them into practice in real time, warts and all, and the next section invites you to share in the lived experience of these stories. May they all act as calls to action.

PART TWO

THE LEADERS AND THEIR JOURNEYS

NOTE: all the featured leaders' articles appeared in *Recruitment International* between June 2014 through to September 2016 and are reproduced here, with in some cases, minor modifications.

For clarity please note that Charlie Walker left Vivid Resourcing in 2016 and Dean Kelly is no longer CEO at Synarbor having successfully led its sale in 2015. Furthermore Alan McBride became Chairman at Camino Partners and Matthew Eames Executive Director at Eames Consulting in 2016.

04 34
STRATEGIC INTENT - VISION

38 **Dean Kelly** CEO - Synarbor plc
42 **Robert Thesiger** CEO - Fiser Group
48 **Jane Lovell** MD - Cooper Lomaz

54 **Alan McBride** MD - Camino Partners
58 **Julie O'Neill** MD - McCall
64 **Darren Ryemill** CEO - Opus Professional
Services Group

05 70
COUP D'OEIL - INTUITION

74 **Sue Cooper** CEO - Morgan Hunt
80 **Scott Bulloch** MD - ATA Recruitment
84 **Mike Gawthorne** CEO - Serocor

90 **Stuart Britton** CEO - RDL Corporation
96 **Paul Jameson** MD - Outsource UK
100 **Greg Latham** MD - Encore Personnel
104 **Pam Easen** CEO - H1 Healthcare

06 108
AUDENTES FORTUNA JUVAT - COURAGE

114 **Toni Cocozza** MD - DP Connect
118 **Charlie Walker** Former CEO
Vivid Resourcing

122 **Adam Shulman** CEO - Simply Education
126 **David Cook** MD - National Locums
132 **Matthew Eames** CEO - Eames Consulting
138 **Andy Hogarth** CEO - Staffline

07 142
INFLECTION POINTS - FORTITUDE

146 **Albert Ellis** CEO - Harvey Nash
150 **Richard Herring** MD - Volt
154 **Michelle Watson** MD - Gemini People
160 **John Hailstone** CEO - Compello
Staffing Group

166 **Karen Silk** CEO - Capital
International Staffing
172 **Jason Stewart** CEO - DRC Locums
178 **Steve Ingham** CEO - PageGroup

08 182
BLUE OCEANS - IMAGINATION

186 **Gary Ashworth** Chairman - Interquest
Group plc
190 **Adam Buck** CEO - Phaidon International
196 **Andrea Williams** MD - Ambition

200 **David Rai** CEO - Testing Circle
204 **Andrew Larholt** CEO - Montash
208 **Joost Kreulen** CEO - Empresaria
Group plc

04

STRATEGIC
INTENT
VISION

W e shall not cease from exploration
And the end of all our exploring
Will be to arrive where we started
And know the place for the first time.

"Four Quartets" TS Eliot

As we saw in the last chapter from Professor Michael Porter's work on strategy, the core of this important concept is to choose to undertake a different set of activities to deliver a unique mix of value.

The choice of activities begins with the first step in any business journey (which provides the fuel to the fire of a great strategy) and that is a vision or purpose, what celebrated business scholars Gary Hamel and CK Prahalad called 'strategic intent' in their seminal article of that title which appeared in the Harvard Business Review in 1989.

HAVING A 'STRATEGIC INTENT' FOR YOUR LIFE OR YOUR BUSINESS MEANS THINKING DIFFERENTLY."

In that article the authors define this core attribute of all successful businesses as the ability of thinking beyond current capabilities and resources you or your company may have and imagining a future that inspires you. So this is not about 'benchmarking'; important as that is, if you limit your business to that then you are an imitator, not an innovator.

Having a 'strategic intent' for your life or your business means thinking differently. To return to Professor Michael Porter's key definition it is to seek to push the boundaries and standards beyond what you currently think possible.

In this chapter we will see how Dean Kelly and Rob Thesiger benefitted from positive catalysts to create a vision that took them beyond their comfort zones.

In Dean's case, notwithstanding years of success as a recruiter in the IT sector, his decision to create an education recruitment business (with just months of experience within that sector) was driven by a vision of what he saw as a market, still in relative infancy and full of opportunity. The spectacular and profitable growth of Dean's business that followed is testimony to the power of that vision.

Rob, having done pretty much everything else as a recruitment leader decided he would take on the one remaining challenge of creating a business from scratch; given this was as a specialist within the ⟩

financial services sector and he chose to do so in the tumult of the post-Lehman financial crisis one could question whether he had lost his mind! But his vision gave him unwavering faith to make it the success that FISER Group has become.

Jane Lovell, for whom recruitment was a second career after a successful track record in medical sales, could see herself creating a truly outstanding business driven by her passion for the highest values in her beloved East Anglia and was prepared to leave the high visibility brand of Hays after just a few years to pursue this vision.

In a similar vein Julie O'Neill, having decided against attending university (much to her father's disappointment), had the vision to see beyond her secretarial role at a recruitment business and identify that the sector offered opportunity suited to her ambition, work ethic and people skills.

Interestingly negative or seemingly negative events can act as a catalyst to create an inspiring vision. Darren Ryemill and Alan McBride, the remaining leaders in this chapter, offer intriguing examples of this.

Darren simply became disenchanted (his own description of his feelings is couched in rather more forthright language) enough to decide to start his own business - after just two years in recruitment - when the MD for whom Darren worked didn't even recognise Darren despite him being a star performer.

Alan McBride, one of the youngest people in the UK to qualify as an accountant, enjoyed great success leading recruitment business

THE CATALYST FOR A COMPELLING VISION CAN COME IN A NUMBER OF FORMS."

Howard Hunterskill (as Managing Director, having been FD) to a successful sale to Modis in 1997. But he had a driving ambition to create his own recruitment business from scratch and roll up his sleeves to drive its growth. He declined the opportunity to work as an FD after the Modis sale instead successfully establishing Balanced People, building it up over the next decade before he then successfully sold it on.

So the catalyst for a compelling vision can come in a number of forms and the key is to harness that energy and transmute it into a purpose that inspires all those that share within it. ⌐

▲ Remember - without vision you perish
▲ Learn to recognise the signs in your career that might act as catalysts to your vision
▲ These can emanate from 'positive' circumstances
▲ They can also come cloaked in the guise of disappointment or set back
▲ Vision will be the tool that helps you overcome the inevitable vicissitudes of business.

04

DEAN KELLY
CEO - SYNARBOR PLC

Dean Kelly is CEO at Synarbor plc, a leading provider of education support and recruitment solutions with a turnover for 2014 of £30 million and approximately 100 employees. A celebrated recruitment leader, he was voted 'Business Leader of the Year' by *Recruitment International* in 2013.

I have left every meeting with him feeling motivated and enriched. His passion is infectious, whether we are discussing matters of political economy or the world of boxing. Today he shares time with political leaders and billionaires. It is a long way from his roots, as Kelly explains.

"I grew up in a tough council estate in North London. Although it was a challenging environment at times, being a local amateur boxer and Chelsea FC schoolboy, always

THE ADVERTS IN THE PRESS THAT OFFERED THE HIGHEST OTES WERE ALWAYS IN RECRUITMENT. SO I APPLIED AND EVENTUALLY JOINED COMPUTER FUTURES IN 1998."

gave me a fair bit of favour. I was also fortunate enough to attend the leading boys' state school in the UK. I loved sport and this exposure to those from a different socio-economic background inculcated a belief that hard work could level the playing field not only in sport but also in life."

Kelly initially thought of becoming a surveyor but saw the long-term rewards were insufficiently motivating. He knew his work ethic was Stakhanovite; he just needed the right opportunity. That opportunity presented itself in the form of the recruitment industry. As Kelly says, *"The adverts in the press that offered the highest OTEs were always in recruitment. So I applied and eventually joined Computer Futures in 1998."*

Despite working longer hours than anyone else *("hard work beats talent every time")* he struggled for the first six months. This might have been due to his doing manual jobs evenings and weekends to supplement his income! A turning point was a meeting with his MD, the legendary Gary Goldsmith. *"I thought I was going to be fired,"* he says. *"I admitted moonlighting. But Gary believed in me and offered a three month salary guarantee. My results exploded. I was fortunate to be at CF at a special time, learning from some of the best recruiters the industry has ever known."*

04

Thereafter Kelly ascended the recruitment ladder at bewildering speed. He moved to Paragon IT and then Dream (now Servoca) where he built its IT and banking/telecoms division to 40 consultants in 12 months! Having spotted an opportunity within the education sector at Dream, Kelly left and founded Kellis in 2002. He recalls, *"Back then the education recruitment market appeared nascent - certainly when compared to IT - and I was happy to disrupt the status quo quite early in its economic life cycle."*

Despite just months within education recruitment, Kelly developed Kellis into one of the fastest growing start-ups to exit recruitment groups in the UK. *"We secured our first contract having only a handful of teachers on our books - always think big! We eventually won 13 major contracts with schools and authorities within 24 months. We also secured a contract with GEMS, the world's largest provider of independent education. Its owner is a billionaire who I approached directly after reading about him in the Economist."*

Kellis was delivering £2.2 million EBIT when acquired by Public Recruitment Group for 6.5 times EBIT - all within three years of starting up! Kelly reveals, *"It was quite a journey! Unfortunately within a few weeks PRG issued a two year profit warning - we had an earnout period so this was a nasty shock - and the next phase of my business education began!"*

Within a few months of finishing his earnout Kelly took over as CEO of the whole group, attracted outside investment to save the business, disposed of failing non-core divisions and de-listed from AIM as the credit crunch hit. Kelly says, *"The outstanding work done by my teams*

Outside of work, Dean channels some of his excess energy with Muay Thai, Boxing and Mixed Martial Arts.

at Synarbor has meant that we now have a business delivering great growth year on year and one which is financially very sound."

Synarbor has gained a superb reputation for its innovative 'TeachIn' managed service, and for being the only agency to work with an LEA to manage a school out of 'special measures' and present data to show high quality 'supply teachers' improve outcomes in schools.

Kelly regularly meets Government Education Ministers to share his ideas. He also nurtures leadership of the next generation of recruitment CEOs, being the co-founder of the Recruitment Directors Lunch Club.

Outside work Kelly is married with three children and channels some of his boundless energy through Boxing, Muay Thai and MMA. He is justly proud of his journey, stressing, *"I came from a tough background but I also believe that true social mobility is possible. It is amazing what can be achieved through hard work, determination and focus. Those gifts are not preserved for an elite; anyone can tap them if they choose."*

Stirring words from Kelly. He has walked his talk and is a beacon of hope for anyone. ⌐

"IT IS AMAZING WHAT CAN BE ACHIEVED THROUGH HARD WORK, DETERMINATION AND FOCUS.

ROBERT THESIGER
CEO - FISER GROUP

Robert Thesiger is chief executive officer of The FISER Group, a UK-based human capital specialist operating solely in the financial services sector. Thesiger's career has been framed within human capital for over 23 years, rising from recruitment consultant to chief executive of a publicly listed global financial services recruitment business, before launching The FISER Group as a start-up.

The Group comprises BRUIN Financial, IBAM Consulting and LUDGATE Search. In 2014 the business delivered over £15 million of turnover, and currently employing more than 50 people, it is on track to more than double this figure by December 2016.

IT WAS COLD CALLING, I LOVED IT AND RAPIDLY BECAME MANAGER OF A TEAM OF 15 PEOPLE."

Having met Thesiger often in recent years one is struck by his eloquent passion for business and a desire to strive for visionary goals. If one were to encapsulate his approach to life it would be audentes fortuna juvat ('fortune favours the bold').

He has a flair for communication and a keen aptitude for business, both of which were evident from a young age. As the youngest of five siblings, his ability to talk his way to attaining his desired outcomes (and/or getting out of trouble) was essential and his business acumen really started during a pre-university gap year in Australia, when Thesiger set up a novelty balloon business which involved him riding a unicycle dressed as a clown. He says, *"I became quite a brand, even appearing on a national TV advert, and grew the business to employ 15 people before selling the concern for a few thousand pounds and returning to London."*

After graduating from Exeter University, Thesiger began his career at Badenoch and Clark in 1993 and quickly established himself, recalling, *"I began with a telephone and phone book, specialising within financial services. It was cold calling, I loved it and rapidly became manager of a team of 15 people."*

After four very successful years, Thesiger took a characteristically surprising but bold decision to indulge his wanderlust and resigned to travel the world again for six months, which included watching a substantial amount of test cricket, a stint following the British and

Irish Lions tour and several weeks sitting on beaches in the Caribbean and South Africa.

Returning to the UK, Thesiger joined Morgan McKinley and over the next decade his recruitment career saw him rise to become managing director and then CEO at the firm, where he played an instrumental role in the successful merger with Imprint plc in 2005. In 2007 Thesiger became CEO of Imprint plc.

Having completed the second sale transaction of his career in 2008, he decided to leave the business in January 2009.

"Having effectively grown and sold the same business twice in three years, it was time to move on to new challenges in my career. I quickly realised that one of the only challenges I had not undertaken within human capital was to engage in a start up," he said.

Working with his plc CFO, Colin Webster, he raised some £1.5 million from private investors, together with their own capital, and BRUIN Financial was born in 2010.

Thesiger stresses, *"This has been the hardest and most demanding thing I have ever done but also the most stimulating. Many people thought we were mad to launch a financial services recruitment business in the midst of the worst recession for a generation and more pertinently, a recession caused by the collapse of the financial services sector. In March 2010 we began with no computers, no furniture and no clients. Nonetheless I knew that we could offer true value to clients, candidates and employees and also differentiate BRUIN within the market place".*

"IT IS VITAL THAT YOU ARE CONSTANTLY EVOLVING YOUR SERVICE OFFERINGS IN ORDER TO MAINTAIN COMPETITIVE ADVANTAGE."

The business has flourished and whilst BRUIN offered traditional permanent, temporary and interim contingent human capital solutions, it was joined in 2013 by IBAM Consulting which specialises in business change consultancy and project management. LUDGATE Search forms the third entity within The FISER Group and helps clients with senior level executive appointments.

"As we came out of the recession, it was important that we recognised how the global financial services landscape had changed and would continue to change," says Thesiger. He adds, "As with most things in business, it is vital that you are constantly evolving your service offerings in order to maintain competitive advantage. The establishment of the FISER Group and its associated businesses was our response to this ever-changing landscape."

However, during this period of growth Thesiger endured a life threatening illness.

He explains, "In early 2012 I became very ill for eight months. Amazingly, it wasn't the result of anything I had done, I was just unlucky! The priest at my bedside was a defining moment and the whole episode changed my perspective on all aspects of my life."

04

Thesiger returned to business in October 2012 and with an even deeper sense of passion and commitment. As he says, *"I decided that I would do everything in my business and personal life to continually improve and take on challenges. I take very seriously FISER's core values of humility, inspiration and pride. I guess the illness made me even more committed to having no regrets."*

At FISER one ground-breaking challenge that Thesiger and his colleagues have grasped with both hands relates to social mobility. Responding to Rt Hon David Lammy MP's lament at the lack of social mobility in the UK, BRUIN Financial launched the City Talent Initiative ('CTI') in 2013.

Thesiger elaborates, *"This is aimed at helping those with talent, but who lack the social capital in terms of connections/networks into the City, to receive support to gain entry into leading City firms. The programme is managed by the Social Mobility Foundation and working with mentors, young talented people gain summer internships and guidance about university choices."*

The initiative has gained cross party political support and last year 30 students gained experience at such firms as Ernst & Young, RBS and JP Morgan. Typically, 85% of those in the programme in London are from ethnic minorities and over 60% are female.

If I may be permitted a personal comment here: I came from a low income, ethnic minority background with no social capital vis-à-vis the City. I recall many talented school friends who could have benefited so much from a CTI type of initiative. Kudos to Thesiger and BRUIN.

Robert rode a unicycle to help sell novelty balloons while on a gap year in Australia and was known as "Bob the Balloon man"!

Outside business Thesiger is a family man, passionate sports fan and total devotee to his mad cocker spaniel, Jessie. He shares his time between London and France where his wife, Zaylie, and young children live.

He enthuses, *"Life is about being bold, creative and having fun. Renovating and rebuilding the house in France is one manifestation of that. Within the human capital arena, it is about understanding that people are truly creative and The FISER Group seeks to accommodate individualism within the matrix of our core mission and values.*

"Without good people who are inspired you have very little. Diversity is a crucial element of this; for example, BRUIN's senior management team is all female and our highest fee earner is a mother of three, who works three days a week. I have long championed flexible working for mums and dads and for all employees to be treated like grownups, not micro-managed as if at primary school."

Thesiger has (literally and figuratively) travelled a long way from his unicycling days and one suspects there remain many adventures ahead of him!

"LIFE IS ABOUT BEING BOLD, CREATIVE AND HAVING FUN.

JANE LOVELL
MANAGING DIRECTOR
COOPER LOMAZ

J ane Lovell is co-founder and managing director of Cooper Lomaz, the multi-sector and award winning recruitment business based in East Anglia, the excellence of which was recently recognised by its inclusion in the 2015 'Sunday Times Best 100 Small Companies to Work For' list.

Joseph Campbell, who was one of the world's leading authorities on mythology, wrote (in his "The Hero with a Thousand Faces") of the near universal myth of a hero who ventures from home to gain lessons and insights but whose journey comes to fruition back in his/her homeland. I am reminded of this whenever

I HAD A BURNING AMBITION TO SUCCEED AND UNDERTOOK IN-DEPTH RESEARCH INTO RECRUITMENT AS AN INDUSTRY."

I have the pleasure of Lovell's company whom I have known for some years.

Her career has taken her across the UK, while her leisure time incorporates trips to St Lucia and Australia each year. However, her soul is forever embedded in Norfolk and East Anglia and Cooper Lomaz has its roots proudly in the area. She says, *"I was born in Norfolk and love this area and indeed East Anglia. I went to school here and represented Norfolk in athletics and that success in sports inculcated a desire to excel in competition as well as imbuing within me a sense of self confidence."*

Lovell decided to plunge into the world of work rather than attending university after completing her A-levels and so began what turned out to be more than a decade of work within the field of science. *"My first role was as a pharmacy technician at Lowestoft hospital in Suffolk. I loved the role as well as the opportunity to receive my training in London."*

It was at that point that Lovell was first exposed to the world of recruitment, a sector which she would of course enter many years later. She explains, *"I was headhunted into the role of medical representative and joined the world-renowned pharmaceutical company Bayer. I sold into GP surgeries and to hospital doctors."*

Having excelled in the position she was later headhunted again to join other leading pharma businesses such as Johnson and Johnson and eventually Roche. Lovell reflects, *"My competitive spirit, forged during*

*my time representing Norfolk in athletics, stood me in good stead. I
also found the role of medical rep intellectually stimulating as I had
to master clinical papers in the relevant medical fields."* In fact, at
both Johnson and Johnson and Roche, Lovell was one of the top five
performers across nationwide sales teams of more than 150 people.

Life was great for Lovell at this point in her career. She was a top
performer with very good earnings and had a generous expense account
alongside a company car; all the accoutrements a young ambitious person
could want! As often happens it was at this stage that destiny intervened
to (eventually) take her down a completely different commercial path.

She explains, *"I had met and married by this time and decided to
join my husband for his posting to Germany (he was in the RAF) and
I embarked on the life as an officer's wife. Cutting a long story short
I could not adjust to that, missed the fulfilment of my career and my
husband being sent to the Gulf War added even more pressure."* Lovell
returned to the UK and unfortunately her marriage ended.

Destiny had another hand to play when she learnt a family friend was
running a successful recruitment business on the south coast, and
it was this friend who suggested Lovell might want to explore this
sector. *"I had a burning ambition to succeed and undertook in-depth
research into recruitment as an industry,"* she says.

Having previously thought about setting up on her own in the medical
sales field she adds, *"I knew by then that I could not easily create
my own medical rep business and realised that recruitment offered
opportunities to be entrepreneurial."* As if guided by a providential

hand she noticed a consultant vacancy for Hays at its Norwich office and was successful in securing the role.

She emphasises, *"The chance to begin a new career in Norwich was wonderful; I was brimming with enthusiasm and just had the self-belief that this would work. This helped me stomach what was in effect a 60% reduction in basic pay compared to my medical rep pay! But very quickly I remember having an epiphany and thinking 'this is for me' and realising that I had found my vocation."*

Within 18 months Lovell was promoted to manager and had also met her future business partner, Charlotte Cooper (also from Norfolk and who had recently joined Hays and went on to run its Colchester office) and they realised that through a set of common values, commitment to long-term business relationships and deep care for candidates that they could create their own recruitment company.

Cooper Lomaz was born in January 1990 in a tiny office in Bury St Edmunds, Suffolk and the rest, as they say, is history.

Explaining how she and Cooper tackled running the company, Lovell tells me, *"We initially focused on the accountancy and finance segments of*

I WAS BRIMMING WITH ENTHUSIASM AND JUST HAD THE SELF-BELIEF THAT THIS WOULD WORK."

the market which is where we had created our initial success as recruiters. Over the years we have branched out to become a true multi-sector partner across East Anglia and encompass eight sectors including engineering, IT, oil, gas and renewables and sales and marketing."

Cooper Lomaz now employs 72 people and at the end of 2014, the highly profitable business had a turnover of £14 million. It operates 'centres of excellence' across its Norwich, Lowestoft and Bury St Edmunds offices and whilst it has traditionally focused on permanent recruitment it has a growing contractor business with some 30% of its business now in that area.

Lovell says, _"Our philosophy centres on being 'right first time' when providing solutions to our clients and we are proud at both the breadth and longevity of client relationships we have developed. That we have done so in a way that helps the economy of East Anglia makes me especially proud. We also offer career opportunities to local people and our team is loyal, knowledgeable and committed."_

This commitment to excellence was recognised earlier this year when Cooper Lomaz was listed in The Sunday Times 100 Best Small Companies To Work For 2015. Cooper Lomaz placed 22nd overall in the UK. _"I am so proud of this recognition,"_ Lovell proclaims.

"That we scored so highly in the categories focusing on being open and honest as management as well as encouraging people to use all their skills is really wonderful. Many of our senior management for example began their careers with us as trainee consultants; that includes our managing director Richard Mould."

FOR THOSE WITH AMBITION AND A DESIRE TO HELP PEOPLE, CANDIDATES AND CLIENTS, IT IS A FABULOUS CAREER FOR YOUNG PEOPLE."

Cooper Lomaz is now extending its operations beyond East Anglia and its team of 60 specialist consultants and more than 25 years of experience provides a perfect springboard for further expansion. With this in mind I took the opportunity to ask Lovell to share some of the key lessons her journey has provided for her to which she obliges, telling me, *"I have set audacious goals and completely focused on their attainment. Hard work and always being guided by strong values have been keys to our success and we have been prepared to invest in the best professional advice we can afford at key junctures along our journey."*

Outside Cooper Lomaz, Lovell has remarried and through her Australian husband (and her sister who lives in Melbourne) regularly spends time with family in Australia and she also has a home in paradisiacal St Lucia which she visits three times a year.

Like the heroic figures of myth her heart remains at home in East Anglia and she exudes the passion and verve that has helped Cooper Lomaz flourish so well. She remains a big believer in the recruitment industry, declaring, *"We are proud to be a local business with world class standards and ethics. I believe in the recruitment sector and it is a shame that many people often simply fall into the sector. For those with ambition and a desire to help people, candidates and clients, it is a fabulous career for young people."*

04

ALAN MCBRIDE
MANAGING DIRECTOR
CAMINO PARTNERS

Alan McBride is Managing Director of Camino Partners, the niche recruiter specialising in sourcing talent for the staffing sector from back office roles to C-suite appointments. Alan has been involved in recruitment for 30 years although he began as a certified accountant. *"I left school at 16 after O levels. I saw an ad for a trainee accountant, had the interview wearing my school uniform and entered the life of work!"*

Alan excelled and qualified in 1981 at just 21, one of the youngest ever to complete the ACCA qualification. One of his first roles was as financial accountant with Playboy in London:

I FELT A LITTLE JADED AND NEEDED A NEW CHALLENGE. I LOVED RECRUITMENT."

"It was a great learning ground for a young accountant requiring strong financial controls and speed of reporting. It was great fun and part of the monthly stock take included counting bunny tails in the bunny changing room," Alan reminisces gleefully!

He entered the world of recruitment in 1984, joining IT recruitment business Hunterskil Group and progressing to financial director in 1987. When he joined the company it had £5 million turnover which grew to £20 million before merging with Howard Organisation (a technical and engineering recruiter) to become a £40 million turnover business, Hunterskil Howard plc.

"This was a subsidiary of Wolseley plc, a FTSE100 company. My experience as FD meant I was financially literate, crucial as part of a large listed business. I was eventually promoted to MD and we grew the business to £80 million turnover by the time of its £55 million sale to Modis in 1997." Alan had clearly done well to be the MD through to the sale of the business.

But he had always keenly felt that as well as having the forensic financial flair he had an entrepreneurial ability as a recruiter. *"It was time to leave after the sale to Modis. I felt a little jaded and needed a new challenge. I loved recruitment. I then chanced on an article about a growing recruitment business (ESS), which needed an FD and I contacted the MD. I was offered the role but eventually declined as I wanted the challenge of my own business. I set up Balanced People in 1998 and ESS became my first client!"*

04

Alan grew Balanced People (which specialised in the recruitment of FDs/CFOs for people based service businesses including private equity backed ones) and placed FDs with well-known recruiters such as Glotel, Reed Health, SBS, MSB and InterQuest. In 2005 he eventually sold Balanced People to Kingston Smith, a top 20 firm of chartered accountants. *"There was a three year earn out period and I am pleased to say I achieved maximum earn out payments and then I decided to take a sabbatical year and that included travel and 'me time'."*

The lure of recruitment proved too strong for this energetic entrepreneur and he set up Camino Partners in 2011 together with partners Sachin Ruparelia and Matt Newman. Alan's network, knowledge and respect within recruitment are clearly a powerful foundation for Camino's growth over the past three years: *"As an ex FD of an £80 million recruitment business (Hunterskil Howard) and also someone who has sold a recruitment business which I created (Balanced People) I am able to deeply understand the needs of recruitment businesses as they source talent not just for immediate operational business needs but also as part of a strategic plan for the growth and development of the business,"* Alan explains.

In March this year Alan was elected a member of the Representative Committee at APSCo, as part of his commitment *"to give something back to the sector that has been so good to me."*

Outside of recruitment Alan is a partner in his wife's residential property franchise business and his love of figures and statistics is realised by his 'hobby' as a participant in tournament poker. *"I enjoy*

Alan McBride plays poker at a serious level and travels all over the world for tournaments

the social aspects of the game as well as the competitive spirit of course and the chance to win some money is never to be devalued. I am currently up over £30k!"

I always enjoy meeting Alan to catch up on the sector and his insights are invaluable; given his expertise and track record, however, I suspect I will resist any temptation to sit opposite him at the card table!

"THE CHANCE TO WIN SOME MONEY IS NEVER TO BE DEVALUED.

JULIE O'NEILL
MANAGING DIRECTOR
MCCALL

Recruitment professionals operate in a pressured climate; never more so than in today's fiercely competitive global jobs market. It is this, perhaps, that makes the Rec2Rec market acutely demanding. This is the arena in which Julie O'Neill has specialised for nearly two decades. She is joint managing director of McCall, one of the largest and well-known Rec2Rec businesses in the UK.

Part of the London Stock Exchange listed Empresaria Group, it specialises in placing the best recruitment talent within the industry's exacting clientele across all levels, and across all the various specialist sectors from IT to FMCG and finance to technical recruiters.

WE TREAT OUR CANDIDATES AND CLIENTS AS WE OURSELVES WOULD WANT TO BE TREATED."

The company is headquartered in the City of London and has offices in Hertfordshire and Singapore, as well as Australia (following its merger with Norris and Partners). O'Neill, who spent more than a decade with Select and Ajilon prior to joining McCall in 1999, focuses on C-Suite appointments within recruitment both nationally and internationally. Nick Bancroft is joint managing director and his 20 years within recruitment include leadership roles with Robert Walters and Alexander Mann.

Upon asking O'Neill to reflect on the Rec2Rec world, she tells me, *"It is a demanding market and we understand that. Nick Bancroft and I have nearly 60 years combined in the recruitment sector!"* She explains, *"We treat our candidates and clients as we ourselves would want to be treated."*

As recruitment has become ever more global, McCall follows its clients' *'talent needs'.*

O'Neill says, *"We pride ourselves on our reputation for ethics and meeting even the most difficult briefs whether a highly niche recruiter in the US finance markets or an oil and gas biller in Kazakhstan."*

O'Neill grew up in Muswell Hill in North London and her father, an immigrant from the Indian subcontinent (who worked in management with JVC and also engaged in property development) was an important influence. She says, *"My father inculcated within me the importance of making a contribution to the nation and striving to realise my full potential. Stereotypically this meant ensuring I went to university."*

04

While in the first year of her A-levels however, O'Neill got a summer job in a publishing house and also used her flair for efficiency helping well known BBC sports journalist and writer Mihir Bose type up his book on the Aga Khan. She then took the bold step to leave education and work full time as an administrator at the publishing house, recalling, *"My father didn't talk to me for two weeks! He was set on my attending university."*

After an uninspiring stint at the BBC working as an administrator (*"There was a lot of clock watching and little dynamism!"*) fate led her to a secretarial job at a recruitment business. Business School theorists (such as William Duggan of Columbia University) highlight the importance of intuition and following one's instinct as a key component of successful leaders. O'Neill trusted her instinct and saw the big picture beyond her secretarial role.

She says, *"I loved the fast pace, people interaction and commercial energy and remember saying to myself that I can do this and so decided on a recruitment career,"* she registered with Select Appointments in 1987 to pursue this and they then turned around and offered her a role as a consultant!

Despite being the youngest in the office she excelled, telling me, *"My passion aligned perfectly with my ethic of hard work. I became the top biller and that remains recruitment's great positive; irrespective of age/background if you deliver results you will be rewarded."*

O'Neill rapidly became the youngest branch manager and later, area manager in London. After eight years, however, she wanted to specialise. *"I saw an opportunity in the accountancy and finance sector,"* she says. *"I was placed with Ajilon - incidentally by the original owner of McCall!"*

O'Neill joined Ajilon in 1996 (reporting directly to the UK vice-president). She worked in its 'Accountants on Call' brand as an area manager in London and the South East. She explains, *"The brand (significant in the US) was on a mission to grow the UK market. We opened an office in St Albans and I worked closely with large blue chip clients including the likes of Citibank."*

After 12 years as a successful recruiter O'Neill's next move was to McCall in 1999 as general manager. She helped to grow the company by establishing a senior appointments division and this despite having to go through a divorce while her two children were just ten and five years old. O'Neill reveals, *"McCall were very supportive to me during this period and supporting staff remains a vital part of our values."*

In 2003 another opportunity to follow her intuition presented itself. As O'Neill explains, *"Rec2Rec businesses are not straightforward to sell. Given the network I had built amongst senior recruitment leaders I handled identifying a strategic acquirer for the business and eventually the sale."* She reached out to Miles Hunt and Empresaria and the deal was done. O'Neill became a joint managing director of the business in 2003.

She says, *"I was delighted with the Empresaria deal and later I placed Tony Martin as NED in the Group. This led to opportunities to serve* recruitment clients across the world. This was crucial as the trend for recruiters to diversify geographically and vertically meant we would be positioned adroitly across international markets."

I asked O'Neill to reflect on the Rec2Rec market in which she has worked since 1999. She said, *"The Rec2Rec market has a variable reputation within recruitment. For McCall there is no magic formula. The key to success was and remains developing powerful networks of course and having deep knowledge of the different segments within recruitment. There is no shortcut to investing the time to develop the brand!"*

"But perhaps most importantly we have trust-based and long standing relationships with exceptional candidates and clients; having such a deep talent pool means our clients are always open to speak with us when they contemplate their strategic hiring initiatives."

There have also been tumultuous economic times since 1999 and O'Neill cautions, *"There will always be cycles within recruitment; it is in the nature of the sector to be disproportionately impacted by economic recessions. Clearly the dot-com bubble bursting in 2000 and the global financial crisis in 2008 brought real dislocation in the sector, especially the latter.*

"Now we see challenges in the oil and gas market as the oil price crashed last year. But given our penetration internationally and across so many verticals we have remained key partners to recruiters who do see growth even in challenging times."

Julie has volunteered as a Samaritan.

Outside of work O'Neill has a busy home life and two grown-up children. Her son (Christian) is at university, while daughter (Jordan) followed in O'Neill's footsteps for a while, working as a City recruiter following her graduation. O'Neill is also stepmother to two grown daughters (Kerry and Jodie) and grandmother to two boys! She and husband Mark (a stamp dealer) also enjoy international travel when they get the chance.

O'Neill has also been an active member of the Church all her life and over the last five years, has volunteered as a Samaritan.

She says, *"I have found that the values of the Church and the importance of sacrificing one's own time to help those in need help to inform my philosophy in life and business."*

She remains one of the best known and connected people in recruitment and has every confidence in McCall continuing to be a leading partner to the national and international recruitment community.

"THE IMPORTANCE OF SACRIFICING ONE'S OWN TIME TO HELP THOSE IN NEED HELP(S) TO INFORM MY PHILOSOPHY IN LIFE AND BUSINESS.

04

DARREN RYEMILL
CEO - OPUS PROFESSIONAL SERVICES GROUP

Darren is CEO and founder of Opus Professional Services Group, an elite parent company to a number of specialist recruitment solutions ranging from IT and engineering to the public sector and energy markets. The group, headquartered in Bristol, expects to exceed £60 million turnover this year and deliver GP of £20 million across its international offices (including Australia, the US and Europe). Darren was *Recruitment International's* 'Entrepreneur of the Year' in 2013 and Opus was placed on the Sunday Times 100 Best Small Companies to Work For the second consecutive year in 2016.

I OFTEN DESCRIBE MYSELF AS ROLLS ROYCE'S WORST EVER EMPLOYEE!"

Meeting Darren it is impossible not be energised given his infectious zest for life and business which started at a young age:

"I grew up in Yate, Bristol and still live nearby. I have always been driven and recall working three paper rounds. I have never been afraid of hard work!"

He attended Birmingham University completing a double honours degree (engineering and commerce), securing sponsorship and a job with Rolls Royce. *"The Rolls Royce graduate training programme provided a really good insight into business. Unfortunately I didn't have much interest in engineering! In the end I was made redundant so Rolls Royce paid me to join and also paid for me to leave. I often describe myself as Rolls Royce's worst ever employee!"*

Whilst at university he remained entrepreneurial setting up an events company and returned to this after Rolls Royce. It did OK *("I didn't have any understanding of creating sustainable sales pipelines.")* and he visited a recruitment company to find temporary work.

"That's how I then got into recruitment. I liked the idea of dictating your own earnings. In any case I thought why not give recruitment a go because in a few months I'll come back to my event management business anyway."

So in 2002 Darren began his 'temporary' recruitment career for a company called Progressive which are part of the SThree Group.

"Almost from day one I loved it. The energy and the meritocratic environment. So my first impressions of recruitment were really positive and actually, probably, formed the basis of how I try and perform in the job even to this day."

Business School scholar Dan Ariely has written widely on the importance of non-monetary forms of motivation as a key to success. In Darren's case, despite a positive start as a recruiter, it was two negative non-monetary related events that led him to set up on his own. *"I was the top performer but was overlooked for promotion in favour of someone else who happened to have been there longer. I felt this was anti-meritocratic so I left. I strongly believe that you should only stay in an environment that supports your ambitions."*

The second event occurred when he joined an IT recruiter where despite being a star performer the MD of the business didn't even recognise him when Darren visited head office. *"I recall thinking I am making a lot of money for this guy and he doesn't even know who I am! It was at that point I decided to become my own boss."*

So in 2004, with just 24 months in recruitment, he set up Recruit360 and with a friend who joined within a few months, they had grown the business to £4 million turnover (employing 14 people) by 2008. This was the point where Darren looked within and realised his vision was not aligned with that of his partner.

"I wanted to grow something really big and he wanted a lifestyle business. Ultimately we did a deal in 2008; I walked away and set up Opus."

WE SAT DOWN ON DAY ONE AND CREATED AN INSPIRING VISION, WROTE IT DOWN AND IT REMAINS OUR GOAL TO THIS DAY."

World renowned Professor Gary Hamel highlights the importance of a compelling vision when creating a truly world leading and differentiated business. Darren concurs:

"I set up Opus Recruitment Solutions in 2008 with Ryan Speed and Nigel Ramana. We sat down on day one and created an inspiring vision, wrote it down and it remains our goal to this day: 'to become a global leader in niche and innovative recruitment solutions'."

The rest is history and one that continues to be written today inspired by the enduring vision above. In 2012 Opus focused solely on IT but since then has diversified both geographically and by vertical. Baltimore was the first non-Opus brand and now delivers over £10 million with specialist focus on senior public sector appointments. Expansion beyond Bristol began in 2013 and the Group now has a global footprint.

Opus' culture and commitment to innovation also help explain its extraordinary growth and its accolades both within and outside recruitment. *"From the outset we brought on really like-minded people. However grand your strategic vision, having the right culture is critical; it is king and I always say culture eats strategy for breakfast. If I look back now, directors and senior managers here are those who started in the early days, have grown with us – given us a real quality core to the business."*

It is this culture that animates the successful expansion internationally. Its Australian business opened in Sydney in late 2014 and now has a headcount of 25!

Part of this success comes down to finding talent that is local to the market and is expert in the relevant vertical market segments. But as Darren explains the secret is: *"We never lose sight of the fact that any of our international businesses are part of the Opus Professional Services Group and what we do well runs through our DNA so we ensured, in Australia, that two of our 'homegrown' consultants - who began as trainees - went out to Sydney so that our culture was a lived reality rather than something entombed in a manual."*

Whilst innovation is constantly, even glibly trotted out by businesses, Darren and Opus are driving real disruptive change within recruitment. *"For example, talentcubed is the first online platform for the serious gamification of recruitment. The super brands of industry (think Microsoft) use gamification as a way of attracting and screening candidates; why should recruitment lag?"*

Additionally, Opus has created a powerful business mapping model called Northstar which is now being used in large consultancy firms to map businesses and ensure continuous improvement. It also has a module that allows for continual assessment for individuals and staff which includes staff reviews, staff assessments and staff appraisals.

Whilst profound changes have happened within recruitment since Darren joined the sector in 2002 he embraces new tools allowing greater granularity of data interpretation and exhorts recruiters never

Darren Ryemill once had a part in the crowd scene in a football film.

to underestimate the value they add. Referring to digital platforms/ job boards he says, *"These are tools helping to connect parties together, but it's how you connect, the quality of info you're sharing and the opportunities you can put forward to clients and candidates that matters."*

Outside of work Darren is a proud father to his three young children and remains very much a part of his local community. His passion for football remains and whilst he no longer plays (*"I'm too fat, too slow, too lazy, too useless so I've taken up golf!"*) he did manage to be in a crowd scene in a Hollywood film called Goal III!

He is also proud to be a founding partner of the Opera foundation. *"This is a charity making a difference to young lives around the world, to raise aspirations and get what we are currently calling 'neets' (not in education, employment or training) out of poverty and into prosperity."*

A truly inspiring journey and I guess that Rolls Royce's loss is the recruitment sector's enduring gain! ⌐

"I STRONGLY BELIEVE YOU SHOULD ONLY STAY IN AN ENVIRONMENT THAT SUPPORTS YOUR AMBITION.

05

COUP D'OEIL
INTUITION

As seen in Chapter 3 military strategy deeply informed and continues to inform much of the subject matter of courses on 'strategy' in business schools today.

A key concept for all successful leaders in recruitment is what 19th century military strategist Von Clausewitz called 'coup d'oeil'. In translation this means literally 'the stroke of an eye' and equates to the ability to adapt quickly to changes in circumstances and use intuition to make rapid decisions. In other words the most beautifully articulated plans (military or business) are likely to face an unaccounted-for factor (or 'chance' as Von Clausewitz called it) which calls for immediate adaptation of the plan.

From the world of business the fall of Lehman would be an example or indeed the current uncertainty triggered by the Brexit vote on 23rd June 2016 which caught financial markets by surprise and whose effects are likely to cause uncertainty for many months if not years.

This ability, coup d'oeil, was described by Von Clausewitz:

"...it amounts simply to the rapid discovery of a truth which to the ordinary mind is either not visible at all or only becomes so after busy examination and reflection." (From *On War*)

The recruitment leaders in this chapter personify this ability which has played an important role in their journeys to the top. Pam Easen, a nurse working 70 hour weeks in Scotland with six children, discovered the gap within the care home sector in that region, there being a shortage of health professionals to help homes deliver their services. From that realisation she launched H1 Healthcare armed with just a 'pay as you go' phone, no computer and oodles of energy!

Similarly Paul Jameson, driven by the desire to achieve, had the vision of creating his own IT recruitment business in the depths of the 1990/91 business, without ever having managed anyone before! And Greg Latham, despite pouring his savings into being part of a management buyout listened swiftly to his inner voice to leave - due to a conflict of values - and create Encore Personnel despite facing the threat of legal action.

But can this art of coup d'oeil or intuition be cultivated or is it reserved for the select few blessed with what seems a mysterious gift? Often intuitive reactions are seen as very different from analytical decision making; the latter usually follows a set process that includes defining the problem, collecting data and creating charts and flow diagrams and deliberating between competing courses of action.

Intuition on the other hand is very different; business scholar Gary Klein, for example, examining decision-making by firefighters in high pressure situations found that they didn't follow the above pattern of evaluating different options. They seemed simply just to act and find the correct solution.

The good news is that Klein has asserted that this 'strategic intuition' can be cultivated. In his book *"The Power of Intuition: How to use your gut feelings to make better decisions at work (2004)"*, he argues that this ability to choose the right course of action develops from 'intelligent memory' and describes it as *"...the way we translate our experience into action."*

In other words, through our experience, experimentation and patterns of thinking there is built up a store of unconscious knowledge that can be called upon seemingly without effort to deliver an 'immediate' answer. And this is a crucially important tool:

"Intuition is an essential powerful and practical tool. Flawed though it sometimes may be, we could not survive, much less succeed, without it."

This ability is demonstrated by both Mike Gawthorne and Stuart Britton in their respective efforts to deliver Change Programmes in their businesses. In Mike's case his intuition told him that he had undertaken too broad a programme too rapidly and that it was threatening to overwhelm his teams; he had the courage to just know it was right to call a halt and adapt the programme into a more manageable transformation of the business model.

Stuart on the other hand despite the growing success of RDL and its life science expertise knew that the time had come to look at every fundamental of the business, strip it to its basics and ensure that the right people were in the right roles to deliver the longer term strategic vision. He could have simply continued enjoying the growth being achieved but intuitively knew that good is always the enemy of great and made the needed changes.

In a different vein Sue Cooper, despite her starred success delivering top billing performances (part-time I may add) at Hays, knew it was time to take on another challenge. And so in the throes of the recession of the early 1990's (these recruitment folks are gluttons for punishment!) started the process of creating a new business for Michael Page from her lounge with the soundtrack of 'Dirty Dancing' playing in the background to keep her young children amused as she set about creating the business plan!

Always remember:

▲ Success leaves clues
▲ Your experience gives you a vast reservoir of knowledge
▲ Trust your intuition and align it to your research

05

SUE COOPER
CEO - MORGAN HUNT

Sue Cooper is chief executive of multi-sector, award-winning agency, Morgan Hunt, which employs more than 230 people across its offices in London, Birmingham and Manchester. With turnover in excess of £92 million and GP above £18 million (2015), it has a market leading position within public sector verticals and a growing private sector business.

Cooper has been chief executive since March 2016, following more than two years as managing director. The current profound transformation in the public sector offers challenges and opportunities to recruiters but a challenge is nothing new for this charismatic leader, whose recruitment career spans 36 years. Rewind to 25 years ago. 1992, in the teeth of recession, saw Cooper join Michael Page to set up Accountancy Additions (now Page Personnel).

MY FRONT ROOM WAS OUR FIRST OFFICE AND WE CREATED THE CLIENT BASE WITH DIRTY DANCING PLAYING IN THE BACKGROUND."

She recalls, *"It was an 18-person start-up with six offices ringing the M25. My front room was our first office and we created the client base with Dirty Dancing playing in the background, to keep my two young children occupied."*

Business Minded From the Beginning

Although as a child, Cooper variously wanted to be a librarian and then a lawyer – she retains a deep love of books – business has always played a part in her world view. *"Growing up in North West London my father was an inspiration, owning his own retail menswear business and being an accountant. He taught me to guess men's suit sizes at a glance and 95% of the time I was accurate."*

Leaving school after her A levels, Cooper joined the Bank of England within its exchange control department, which, she admits, was very different from the buzzing world of recruitment. *"The job was interesting but the ability to influence was about zero – it was heavily process driven,"* she says. *"The consolation was a fantastic social scene with jugs of G+T at lunch time for about £1".*

She was made redundant after four years, following repeal of the Exchange Control Act, and stumbled into recruitment, where she had an epiphany: *"I joined Hays as a stop gap following redundancy and within weeks had fallen in love with my job: Temp controller, Moorgate* office – fast and furious finance recruitment". Cooper was hired by industry legend Denis Waxman and recalls a different recruitment world to that of today: *"There was zero compliance, no CVs, no PSLs. Basically, the Wild West. But so much fun and very lucrative."*

A Family vs Career Crossroads

Cooper later took four years out to start a family and returned to Hays on a part-time basis, working three hours a day, but she soon reached a crossroads. *"After three months I had made no money,"* she says. Denis Waxman asked to see me and said it wasn't working. I pushed for one more month and said if I hit my target we carried on and if I didn't, we would part company. I doubled my target that month and the rest is history." She enjoyed tremendous success as the only part-time consultant (and number one biller, then working just four hours a day!) later becoming regional manager in the UK. She never worked past 4 pm in order to be there for her children after school, even with eight branches to manage. She reflects, *"I achieved a balance between career and commitment to my children. No mobiles, no emails but I could fill a job on my landline whilst peeling the spuds."*

After eight successful years with Hays, she made the move to Michael Page in January 1992 and whilst the early years of recession were a challenge she grew Accountancy Additions successfully. She eventually led the London and South East Page Personnel Finance business, responsible for more than 100 staff and delivering a GP of £12 million. Her nearly two decades at Page helped hone her obvious gift for business and leadership. *"It was a tough environment which always challenged you to improve,"* she reveals. "I worked with some

I WORKED WITH SOME FANTASTIC PEOPLE AND SAW TRULY TALENTED HIRES ACHIEVE THEIR POTENTIAL."

fantastic people and saw truly talented hires achieve their potential. My boss at the time had two rules; rule #1: work hard; rule #2: work harder"!"

Running a Recruitment Business

It was in late 2011, as Cooper was enjoying her career success at Page, that Terry Benson (ex Michael Page CEO) called. He was chief executive at Morgan Hunt and said he needed a winner to lead the education business: *"I met him at the office, walked in and felt the buzz, energy and passion pouring out of the walls and that was it. I loved running the education, housing and health divisions. Clients were so interesting and the people development hugely satisfying."* Cooper hit the floor running and rapid promotion followed, first to managing director in 2013 and then to chief executive in March this year. She says, *"The CEO role has come late in my career. It had never been my aspiration. I have however thrived under the responsibility. I have always known I could run sales teams but now I know how to run a business."*

'Know how to run a business' ...talk about understatement! Morgan Hunt has grown rapidly, jumping from £66 million turnover in 2013 to £92 million two years later. Accolades have flooded in, including RI's own Best Recruitment Company to Work For - £40-100 million in 2015, even as Cooper has faced significant challenges outside work: *"Losing my father in September 2014 was very tough. I have also lost*

05

my mother-in-law, moved house (after 30 years!) acquired two more grandchildren (I now have three – Max, Ruby and Sophie), nursed my husband Steve through spinal surgery and had shingles! As they say 'what doesn't break you makes you stronger'."

Embedded Culture

Perhaps as noteworthy has been the outstanding initiatives Morgan Hunt has delivered in terms of employee engagement and culture; significant given talent attraction remains perhaps the key challenge to deliver growth for the industry. Cooper stresses, "We strive to create an enviable work culture. Our initiatives go beyond traditional recruitment engagement techniques. We have a 5-strong marketing team with one person dedicated solely to employee engagement." The results have been impressive. There has been more than a 20% increase in headcount since 2014 and 50% female workforce with 46% female director representation. Remarkably, 56% of total hires are through referrals, with a 95% retention rate for such hires, while 73% of current managers joined without any recruitment experience!

Outside of work, Cooper is kept busy by her family. She and husband Steve (they celebrate their Ruby wedding anniversary next year) are proud parents to daughter Michelle (recruitment manager at Tesco) and son Richard (who has his own design business). She also juggles time between doting on her three grandchildren, spoiling Frank (her beloved Shih Tzu), supporting Arsenal and admits to a penchant for shopping!

Notwithstanding the profound changes disrupting the recruitment sector since Cooper first entered it – most notably over the past decade or so with technological advancements – she remains resilient. She declares, *"Fundamentally, we are still a people industry and we are still as strong as ever as a profession. People need people, not algorithms, to help them make crucial decisions in their life."* Following the recent 'Brexit' Referendum and continuing funding constraints vis-à-vis the public sector (particularly pertinent to Morgan Hunt), Cooper also sounds a note of hope amidst the inevitable current uncertainty: *"Despite more than 30 years, three recessions and 360 instances of 'what are we going to bill this month' recruitment to me is still the best job in the world."* ⌐

"WE STRIVE TO CREATE AN ENVIABLE WORK CULTURE. OUR INITIATIVES GO BEYOND TRADITIONAL RECRUITMENT ENGAGEMENT TECHNIQUES.

SCOTT BULLOCH
MANAGING DIRECTOR
ATA RECRUITMENT

Scott is currently managing director of ATA Recruitment (one of the UK's leading white collar engineering and technical recruiters) which is part of RTC Group. Its headquarters is the Derby Conference Centre which is where I met Scott over lunch to learn of his journey within the world of recruitment: *"I had completed an MSc specialising in environmental control. I toyed with the idea of a career in science but mainly due to friends who went into recruitment I decided to investigate that sector and secured a role with ATA in 1997."*

It was a baptism of fire and at first Scott admitted that he had second thoughts and with refreshing candour confessed much self-doubt: *"It was a very sales-orientated*

MY EARLIER EXPERIENCE TAUGHT ME THE VALUE OF STRONG RELATIONSHIPS WITH CLIENTS. THOSE RELATIONSHIPS HAVE ALLOWED US TO BOUNCE BACK."

culture and during the first 13 weeks I often questioned whether I could cut it. I think there was a significant fear of failure." Eventually Scott's professional commitment and focus lead to success and recognition.

He was promoted to manager at ATA's Manchester branch and shortly after making that the most profitable office was promoted once again to start from scratch ATA's rail recruitment business in Derby. Scott recalls, *"This was literally a blank sheet of paper job. No database and no client base. Strategy, processes, operational direction was left to me to formulate. No pressure!"* It was a challenge and one to which he responded superbly. Within the first 18 months he had created a business generating £1.8 million in NFI (Net Foreign Investment).

This was all permanent recruitment and then due to significant challenges with Railtrack the business faced a crisis: *"It was summer 2003 and Railtrack was put into administration and Network Rail was formed as a not for profit business to control the UK rail network. This was a significant period of uncertainty and the large scale renationalisation resulted in ATA losing 65% of its rail business almost overnight! It was a profound learning experience; it taught me the value of having diverse revenue generation streams and also to have less concentration in client base."* He refocused energies and rebuilt the rail business.

In 2006 he was then tasked with establishing a construction recruitment business from scratch too, which within a year or so had grown to 10 staff. They say lightning doesn't strike twice but: *"The global financial crisis of course profoundly impacted all of recruitment and within construction the market froze at the end of Q1 2008. There was massive margin pressure from clients and across the company we had to reduce staff levels by 50%. Our rail business was relatively less impacted. But my earlier experience taught me the value of strong relationships with clients. Those relationships have allowed us to bounce back."*

In 2010 Scott was promoted to head of operations across all markets of ATA Recruitment. Understanding the distinct dynamics of a regional recruitment business (which include it being more transactional new business led than client account managed) Scott helped ATA grow its PBT 72% during 2010-2012. He has also ensured that the business developed a significant contract division which now represents almost half of NFI (Net Foreign Investment).

In February 2012 his results were further rewarded with his appointment to his current role as managing director: He says of his development, *"The business has continued to grow and we have a team of 62 consultants across our branch network. We expect to hit our 2014 budget numbers including generating a turnover in excess of £24 million. Our aim is to double the size of the business within the next 24 months."*

The business offers clients depth of expertise across its range of niche sectors including general engineering, manufacturing and transport, as well as the built environment and infrastructure. Scott has also established an in-house training academy and brand called *"LEap"* which helps the professional development of both new recruiters and top performers. Despite having ambitious growth plans for ATA, Scott manages to balance work and life commitments: *"I have maintained my interest in sport and am a keen golfer but these pursuits definitely come second to a busy family life and three daughters all aged under 10 which keeps me very grounded!"*

He also confesses a developing interest in potentially completing a Triathlon in the near future. Should be 'no sweat' for someone who clearly thrives in the face of a challenge!⌐

"I HAVE MAINTAINED MY INTEREST IN SPORT AND AM A KEEN GOLFER BUT THESE PURSUITS DEFINITELY COME SECOND TO A BUSY FAMILY LIFE AND THREE DAUGHTERS ALL AGED UNDER 10 WHICH KEEPS ME VERY GROUNDED!

MIKE GAWTHORNE
CEO - SEROCOR
GROUP

Mike Gawthorne is CEO of Serocor Group which comprises a group of recruitment and talent management companies including Optamor, Bloc, Hawker Chase, Serocor Solutions and ARM, which he joined in 2000. Its Group businesses encompass permanent, temporary, executive search, L & D and MSP/RPO functions for UK and international clients. With six offices in the UK and headquartered in Havant, Hampshire, it employs more than 200 people.

Meeting Gawthorne at Serocor's prestigious new London offices in Old Broad Street's Tower 42, I can definitely

IN CERTAIN SOCIAL SETTINGS AS A SINGLE MAN, EXPLAINING I WORKED FOR A BUSINESS CALLED 'MATCHMAKER' DREW CURIOUS LOOKS OCCASIONALLY."

appreciate the breath-taking vista over the City that the location affords; what an environment to work in! Now, more than 15 years after joining ARM, Gawthorne is happy to share what the key to the success of the business has been. When asked, without hesitation he says, *"Trust, transparency and fairness to all our people."* His comments chime with the latest findings from the business school world. Professor of Behavioural Economics at Harvard, Matthew Rabin has spent 20 years establishing the principle that 'fairness' pays off; people reciprocate in kind to those who are fair to them.

"Our business is built on empowerment; we have a clear five-year plan and I am committed to helping the MDs of our individual businesses grow and also attract talented people who have ambition that can be developed through the vast experience of the Serocor Board," Gawthorne says. Hampshire born and bred, he has a deep affinity with the county and lives in Wickham with his wife Lucy and their three young sons.

"I have sometimes favoured practice over theory; I was always fascinated by mechanical objects, pulling them apart and re-constructing them," Gawthorne explains of his formative years. He admits to not being a gifted student but his love of sales and business

was sparked early on, as he says, *"I was quite poor academically but managed to claw my way into college to study engineering and eventually to university, earning my BEng degree. But sales were a love from childhood."* He attributes this to his late father who had taken the risk of setting up his own property management company.

Keen for a job in engineering sales after graduating in 1997, Gawthorne visited a recruitment agency (then Matchmaker Personnel and later to become Matchtech Group) who saw his potential and persuaded him that joining them might be the right career move. *"I was interviewed by Adrian Gunn (then a perm manager) and George Materna (who founded Matchmaker and is now non-executive deputy chairman). What I loved was the prospect of the OTE; they promised me rewards that would be commensurate with my effort. I took the 'risk' - my friends from university were all on much higher salaries and after speaking to my father, we both recognised the potential of a sales-based opportunity."*

Gawthorne grew the contract business and thrived; albeit, *"In certain social settings as a single man, explaining I worked for a business called 'Matchmaker' drew curious looks occasionally,"* he jokingly explains. It was at this point that tragedy struck with the unexpected loss of his father at 53. *"My dad was my best friend and role model. He had, I felt, yet to complete his journey and his loss made me step back and look within myself. He was a man with morals, courageous enough to make tough decisions always based on a philosophy of integrity."*

Gawthorne decided making money was less important than creating a legacy in his business life. He decided to take a few months out, during which time he met Paul Huntingdon who had founded ARM in 1996 and remains on the board at Serocor Group. *"At the time ARM focused solely on technology. Paul understood my values, believed in me and, took the leap of faith and asked me to be part of the business. Joining in April 2000, aged 24, my challenge was to create an engineering recruitment business from scratch."*

When he joined, ARM had five people and over the next decade Gawthorne progressed well, becoming operations director in 2003 and managing director in 2007. During this period the business grew to 125 people and over £100 million in turnover. *"After five years of growth, in 2005, we took on an external VC shareholder, Barclays Ventures. They stayed with us until 2007 and the discipline instilled in me by them, in terms of maintaining financial and operational progress, was invaluable."* As the storm clouds began to gather ahead of the global financial recession Barclays sought an exit. Consequently, the management team (including Gawthorne) backed themselves and through a debt-funded MBO took back full control of the business.

Notably 2008-13 was an exceptional period as during the recession ARM bucked the trend and grew in spite of a stalled economy. Gawthorne elaborates, *"Due to the depth of our relationships with clients (some had been with us since I joined ARM in 2000) and the nature of some of the sectors within which we had created a great reputation - such as utilities and defence - we prospered during an otherwise bleak period for the recruitment sector."* Between 2008-2013 the ARM business grew from £75 million to £100 million turnover and tripled profitability!

05

Notwithstanding this striking performance there followed a challenging period. In fact, Gawthorne describes the past 24 months as *"my most challenging"* in the business as it grew very rapidly (hiring-wise and in opening new offices in London, Bristol, Aberdeen and Coventry) and undertook a radical change programme.

"By 2013 I had drafted our five-year strategy, we had Miles Hunt (the current chairman) join the board and we set out a very rapid transformation of the business from a single site, single market (UK) business to one which was multi-sited, multi-branded and internationally focused; all in a matter of months!"

Gawthorne admits this was too much too fast, deeply affecting the culture of the business. He says, *"We underestimated the impact this would have on our people. But when we realised the impact (and given our core values), we admitted our mistake and through maintaining open communications, we now have a fully aligned and wonderful team. We did the hard work to protect and nurture our culture."*

As Joan Magretta (in her 2011 book What Management is: How It Works and Why It's Everyone's Business) says, *"Culture building is hard work. It requires communication, communication and then more communication."* After consolidating the business in the couple of years following 2013, Serocor Group is set for continued growth and expects to hit £120 million turnover in 2015/16. Its range of services underpins this confidence. *"Offering a balanced portfolio of solutions to our clients is critical to our vision,"* says Gawthorne.

Fundraising is high on Mike's agenda and he cycled 300 miles to raise money for a local hospice.

"In addition to perm and contract services (through ARM) we can partner with clients to manage all their talent requirements (via Optamor) and also offer dedicated executive search expertise (via Hawker Chase)."

Outside of work Gawthorne is very much a family man and he and his three sons are all unabashed 'petrol heads' with an enthusiasm for cars and bikes! He also realises the importance of giving back to the community and fundraising is high on his agenda. He recently took part in a 300-mile cycling challenge along with some of his Serocor colleagues, raising a substantial amount of money for a local hospice.

Gawthorne is clearly driven by his vision for the future of the business but has learned key lessons from the past, as he says, *"The board and I are completely dedicated to helping our people realise their full potential. I have not forgotten the opportunity Paul Huntingdon offered me when I was 24 and I want to ensure anyone with the drive and ambition to succeed is afforded the same chance I had to reach their full potential."*

It is also clear that the values of integrity and trust, derived from his late father and role model, are the elements that give Gawthorne his confidence about the business and people within it. ⌐

"I WANT TO ENSURE ANYONE WITH THE DRIVE AND AMBITION TO SUCCEED IS AFFORDED THE SAME CHANCE I HAD TO REACH THEIR FULL POTENTIAL.

05

STUART BRITTON
CEO - RDL
CORPORATION

Stuart Britton is chief executive officer of RDL Corporation which, through its SEC Recruitment and SEC Pharma businesses, provides talent into the life sciences markets in the UK, Europe and Asia via its clinical, commercial and IT divisions. Employing over 70 people, its turnover this year is expected to exceed £21 million and generate over £6.5 million in GP.

I met Britton at RDL's fabulous new City headquarters in Moorgate. Now in his 19th year in recruitment, Britton is keen to dispel the myth of recruiters being purely driven by financial gain. Illustrating this, he says, *"The two major moves in my recruitment career both involved taking a 30% pay cut!"* he laughs. *"I bought into*

I BOUGHT INTO THE VISION AND VALUES EACH MOVE OFFERED. TODAY, MORE THAN EVER, I BELIEVE VALUES ARE A DIFFERENTIATOR IN THIS CROWDED SECTOR."

the vision and values each move offered. Today, more than ever, I believe values are a differentiator in this crowded sector."

The seminal business book, Good to Great, by Jim Collins, details the characteristics that define great businesses. Somewhat counterintuitively, a key factor is style of leadership, personified by a self-effacing and even humble CEO. Britton exudes such traits and seems to thrive in a VC-backed business in a competitive market which is a far cry from his early working life. As he tells me. *"I completed one year of A-levels and then drifted into various jobs. It was when my now wife Sarah and other friends were taking graduate jobs after completing university that I had a career wake up call."* After 135 job applications, he managed to secure three interviews and entered the world of FMCG as a field sales person.

In 1998, nearly four years later (working 15 hours a day and driving over 70,000 miles in the final nine months) an advert caught his attention. *"It featured a TVR sports car and highlighted an OTE of £60k. At the age 26 I was sold on the challenge and took an initial 30% pay cut on the package before commission."* He joined MSB as a contract IT recruiter in the Visual C++ market and found his vocation. *"It was a tough sales-orientated environment,"* he says. *"There were times I doubted myself but I knew it was time to step up or step out.*

Eventually I grew my contract base, delivering billing around £500,000 pa."

At this point, in late 2000, Britton reflected on his long term career prospects, *"I knew I could sell... But I also knew that I could be a leader of a recruitment business"*; and left to join Harvey Nash where his first management role was to rebuild the contract department of Tech Partners to integrate it in the Harvey Nash contract division. He tells me, *"I was then invited to become a manager within Mortimer Spinks - part of Harvey Nash - with full responsibility for the contracts and managed accounts divisions. I grew the contracts division by 30% in 2002, with responsibility for a team of 15."*

Clearly Britton was thriving as a leader at Harvey Nash but opportunity came knocking in the form of RDL Corporation. Within six months, he was running both Computer Personnel and SEC Recruitment. The job move didn't come without risk though. *"I could see the potential opportunity and again took a cut in salary. This time I also took the opportunity to invest all my savings for a small stake in the business,"* Britton reveals.

The following years were a mixture of opportunity and challenge and also saw the growth of the SEC Pharma division. The SEC business developed excellent brand recognition, a notable statistic being that over 70% of clients use its services year on year. The next stage in SEC's evolution came between 2008-2010; Britton explains. *"Mobeus Equity Partners had tracked the business. Their backing of the business was predicated in part on our growing in 2009; this was not exactly a propitious time for recruitment businesses growing! But we*

YOU MUST MAINTAIN UNSWERVING FAITH TO PREVAIL. AND AT THE SAME TIME HAVE THE DISCIPLINE TO CONFRONT THE MOST BRUTAL FACTS OF YOUR CURRENT RESULTS, WHATEVER THEY MIGHT BE."

managed to deliver it!" Britton, along with CFO Nigel Gardner, led the MBO of the business in late 2010 and the past few years have witnessed a transformation in the culture and structural focus of SEC, including expansion in Switzerland, Germany and Singapore.

One of the key characteristics of great businesses identified in Good to Great is the ability to confront reality. The book asserts, *"You must maintain unswerving faith to prevail. And at the same time have the discipline to confront the most brutal facts of your current results, whatever they might be."* Britton affirms this important advice. *"We had to face the huge contraction in our pharmaceutical sector during the 2012-13 period which saw our GP from Clinical Research Organisations fall from £1.5 million pa to £0.5million. But we have also stepped back and questioned every aspect of the business to focus on our key differentiators."*

Clarifying what is often a cliché in business, author Jim Collins in Good to Great advises that, *"People are not your most important asset. The right people are."* Britton agrees, stressing, *"Loyalty repays itself. Three of my directors have been with the business for more than 10 years. We have supported colleagues through tough times and we are proud to also have some 15% of our workforce working flexibly."*

Britton has taken tough decisions to ensure the right people are leading the biggest opportunities. He and his team have focused on successful re-branding and optimising training and development across the business. He has sought clearly to define the strategy of the business and has enlisted external support from Nicholas Watkins of Q4 Management Limited, who has been a vital partner to Stuart since 2014.

These efforts are now bearing fruit. In 2015, the business delivered £18 million turnover and GP of £5.2 million. In 2016 it expects these to grow to £21 million and £6.5 million respectively. The business (split equally now between perm and contract segments) continues to be international, with 30% of revenues being generated in the UK and 65% in Europe. Values remain at the heart of Britton's vision for SEC. Diversity is particularly valued: 65% of employees are female and some 27 languages are spoken in the office. *"I personally run a 'living our values' session - comprising truth, honesty, integrity and commitment - with every single person that joins SEC. It really is that important."*

Outside business, Britton and wife Sarah are proud parents to their two daughters and he divides his time between London and Cheltenham whilst remaining a lifelong West Bromwich Albion supporter.

Having entered recruitment in 1998 (and been with SEC since 2003) Britton is testament to the rewards available to those prepared to work hard and invest time to become true recruitment professionals. His philosophy of why he loves the sector so much is a simple yet powerful one. *"Recruitment is so much more than earning a fee; it's enhancing people's lives. Our work can involve relocating a senior professional with his/her family across continents for the right opportunity. When you do this well there can be few more fulfilling careers. It's as simple as that."*

Britton requested that he take this opportunity to say thank you to so many that have helped him build SEC. From his past and present team, his directors, wider management team, Mobeus Private Equity, Iain Livingston - chairman, Nick Watkins and last but by no means least, his business partner, Nigel Gardner for putting up with him for so many years.

He concludes, *"Without everyone, I would not be the person I am today."*

"RECRUITMENT IS SO MUCH MORE THAN EARNING A FEE; IT'S ENHANCING PEOPLE'S LIVES.

05

PAUL JAMESON
MANAGING DIRECTOR
OUTSOURCE UK

Paul Jameson, is MD of Outsource UK, the award winning national IT and engineering recruitment business he founded over 23 years ago. Paul Jameson thrives on challenges. That is my conclusion after sharing time with him on a number of occasions over the past couple of years. He set up an IT recruitment business without ever having managed anyone before, with no money and in the depths of the recession of 1991; oh - and he likes the odd stroll on mountains and has recently climbed both Mount Kilimanjaro and Toubkal Mount (Morocco)!

I HAVE ALWAYS KNOWN THAT I WANTED TO RUN MY OWN BUSINESS."

I met Paul at Outsource's HQ in Swindon and it seems entrepreneurship is built into his genes. Paul explains, *"My father ran his own business, a newsagent and post office, and from an early age I have always known that I wanted to run my own business. Nothing specific in terms of what sector but just an inner certitude that I would be my own boss one day."*

After completing a diploma in Computer Studies in the mid-1980s Paul worked in the IT sector in Swindon for a couple of years and eventually was placed as an IT contractor with Northern Foods. It was here that he took the first brave/unexpected turn in his working life. *"I enjoyed being an IT contractor but I knew I wanted more in my life. That desire was there and intuitively I decided to join the recruitment business that had placed me on my contract. It was a completely unknown quantity in terms of sector but I decided to try it,"* he says.

Over the next three years or so he worked with two recruiters within the IT sector and thrived. By this time (1990/91) there was a recession and the inevitable pressure to sell grew. Paul stepped back and took another brave decision.

He states, *"My values and ethics have always been focused on building long-term relationships based on trust and confidence. I felt there was a need for such an approach within the IT recruitment space. In the three years I had worked as a recruitment consultant I had eight managers(!) and de facto built a foundation of success through the freedom I had. So I decided that I would take the risk and formed Outsource."*

It is important to recall the courage of this leap. Paul had, despite success as a consultant, never actually managed anyone and had no financial backer for his venture. He funded the business himself for 6 months and began with a tiny office in Swindon and even had to borrow a computer to get started! The rest they say is history but to paraphrase Jon Motson's line, the history of Outsource has been a story of two halves.

"Prior to 2003 we were a small business that grew steadily from inception in 1991 and then had to weather the awful recession at the start of the new millennium," Paul explains candidly. But built on foundations that eschewed hyperbole in favour of traditional principles of integrity (and always seeking to evolve and be accountable), Outsource UK, since 2003, has enjoyed an exceptional trajectory of success. *"The last decade or so has seen myself, my team and the business mature and continually evolve. We have made acquisitions (the first in 2006 and then two in 2011/12) which have enabled the business to have a growing national footprint with offices in Swindon, Manchester, the Midlands and a satellite office in London. In addition, this strategy has permitted us to diversify to encompass expertise in engineering too."*

The numbers for the business tell the dramatic story. In 2003 Outsource UK had a turnover of £2.3 million, in 2008 it stood at £19 million and in 2013 (amidst the most profound recession in generations) it topped £36 million.

"It is however not all about the numbers. One of my greatest fulfilments is helping our staff develop and create a shared ethos that values quality," Paul adds.

Paul has climbed both Mount Kilimanjaro and Toubkal Mount (Morocco).

This commitment is evidenced by Outsource UK receiving the highly respected ISO 9001 accreditation and also a Gold Standard Audit status from the REC. The business also added weight to its Board in early 2014 through the appointment of Charles Hughes as non-executive chairman, who has over of 40 years' experience within IT, including senior roles at ICL and HM Government.

Paul reflects, *"I have learned from the numerous business cycles Outsource has traversed. I think the commitment to long-term relationships and core values has been important as has been my father's advice to work harder and longer than others."*

One can see Outsource continuing to climb the peaks of success... with its founder adding a few mountain summits along the way!

"ONE OF MY GREATEST FULFILMENTS IS HELPING OUR STAFF DEVELOP AND CREATE A SHARED ETHOS THAT VALUES QUALITY.

GREG LATHAM
MANAGING DIRECTOR
ENCORE PERSONNEL

Greg is the co-founder and MD of Encore Personnel, the fast-growing 'blue collar' industrial recruiter.

I met Greg at the swanky GNH Bar in London. This boy from Brum is a football fan (lifelong Villa supporter for his sins) but has the build of a rugby player and a calm and welcoming manner; the proverbial gentle giant!

Recruitment at the Raw End

Greg celebrates 30 years in recruitment next year and began with a high street recruiter in Nottingham.

"Back then it was a very different world and I was often asked to supply 'only females' or 'no blacks'. My focus was

MY FOCUS WAS ALWAYS ON SUPPLYING THE BEST CANDIDATE FOR THE ROLE AND IT IS IMPORTANT NOT TO FORGET THOSE UNENLIGHTENED DAYS."

always on supplying the best candidate for the role and it is important not to forget those unenlightened days and that we have, as an industry, come a long way."

He worked hard (12 hours+ days and 7:30 am starts) and became a manager for the company. He joined Staffline in 1987, then a fledging business doing £1 million turnover. His hard work, people skills and focus saw him rise up the ladder and 13 years later he was Operations Director and the business was delivering a turnover of £27 million.

Opportunity Out of Crisis

It was at this point that Greg had the opportunity to be part of a private equity backed buy out of the business. He saw it as a great opportunity and invested his money and worked with four external managers who were buying in (a 'BIMBO' in the jargon). Unfortunately, he couldn't have predicted what followed:

"I had a young family and was passionate about the business and having an equity stake motivated me enormously. A business is also about values and shared vision; in fact, it's the glue that holds a recruitment business in particular - which has no 'tangible assets' and does not manufacture anything - together for the long term. Unfortunately, there was a profound conflict in values between myself and the incoming team."

Due to this conflict there was a deep impact on morale and there was staff exodus. *"I had reached a cross road in my life. I decided to take the plunge and begin my own business with my co-founders and Encore was born. But it was the darkest time of my life; there was litigation with my former business and it felt as if Encore would be stillborn. Fortunately, we reached a settlement and then decided to do whatever it took to make Encore work for us, our staff and our clients."*

No Looking Back

Determined to ensure that the he would always value people at the centre of Encore, Greg set up the business to give all a stake in its success.

"From our very early days we wished to re create the partnership ideals similar to John Lewis Partnership. So we set up an employee share ownership scheme. Therefore, everyone who works for Encore owns Encore and we believe this means that they really care about the service and experience we give our customers. We think that this makes the Encore difference."

Today Encore, whilst branded as a 'blue collar' specialist, is experiencing growth in vertical markets such as Renewables and energy. It is a business that places 2,800 workers each week, is smashing its budget forecast for 2014 and expects to deliver £48 million turnover by the end of 2016 and employ more than 130 people across its eight locations.

Encore has enjoyed a wealth of accolades including the Best Company to Work For at REC/IRP 2013 awards. Greg is a respected leader within recruitment and sits on the executive committee of ALP as well as being a non-exec Director with the REC. One of the personal highlights for this successful entrepreneur and proud father of three teenage boys was recognition from Richard Branson:

"Encore was honoured as one of the fastest growth companies in the UK and it was a pleasure to personally be invited to Richard Branson's house in Oxfordshire as part of this recognition."

Not bad for a boy from Brum! ⌐

"A BUSINESS IS ALSO ABOUT VALUES AND SHARED VISION; IN FACT, IT'S THE GLUE THAT HOLDS A RECRUITMENT BUSINESS TOGETHER.

PAM EASEN
CEO - H1 HEALTHCARE

Pam Easen, founder and chief executive of H1 Healthcare, a leading international nursing recruitment business, providing permanent and temporary staff as well as training and healthcare services including complex care and occupational health. I often meet Pam in the City of London and have had the privilege of getting to know this extraordinary entrepreneur.

A business owner, a former nurse and mother of six, her journey is utterly fascinating. *"I was brought up in Liverpool and after leaving school at 16 and working for a few years in different industries I began training as a nurse at Liverpool Royal Infirmary. I later moved to Birmingham and married my husband in 1978 and our first child arrived two years later."*

GROWING A BUSINESS IS LIKE NURTURING A BABY - YOU HAVE TO LEARN TO LET GO AT THE RIGHT TIME."

The following decade saw Pam own and sell three care homes, each one increasingly large, add a further five children to the family and move to rural Aberdeenshire where, in the early 1990s, she worked as a self-employed nurse while her husband, Ron, became a pedigree sheep breeder. *"Buying our first care home happened quite by accident. I visited my bank manager to pay off a £100 overdraft. We started chatting about my profession and he suggested that the bank would help me fund a care home if I found some money to invest. We bought our first care home in 1983, a four-bedroomed house, and then continued in the sector for the best part of a decade."*

While working as a self-employed nurse in Aberdeenshire in 2002, Pam spotted a gap in the market which drew on her extensive expertise of the care home sector. *"I realised that care homes needed a lot of care assistants and so I took the plunge to set up a staffing business which did just this. I worked extraordinarily long hours as I was also continuing my role as a self-employed nurse to bring in funds. But with wonderful support from my husband, who helped to look after our six children, I made it work."* The odds seemed to be stacked against Pam. She didn't have a PC, laptop or office and had a pay as you go mobile phone to arrange placements.

What Pam did have was a vision for the business - initially called Premier Care - that she wanted to run and the values and ethics it should have. Over the past 12 years, H1 Healthcare has blossomed into a major nursing recruitment and training business with offices in Aberdeen, Glasgow, Australia and India. It operates throughout the UK and also in the Gulf region and New Zealand. Its clients include the NHS, voluntary organisations, care homes and prisons.

H1 Healthcare was on target to deliver £8 million in turnover in 2014, with 25 staff including its Board of Directors. Pam has grown with the business and learnt to lead as well as manage. She has also strengthened H1's board as it expands internationally.

"Growing a business is like nurturing a baby - you have to learn to let go at the right time. The biggest part of our success is bringing the right people in. It's important they have a passion for caring and for me, as the chief executive, to support them in their role. Learning to delegate took some time for me to get used to. As it was my company I was scared of letting go but it is absolutely vital."

H1 is still a family-owned business and its management team includes Pam's eldest son, Sam, whose leadership is driving the Sydney office, operations director Jay Sihota, who has more than a decade of healthcare and recruitment experience, and financial director Alan McKenzie. Pam recently gave a compelling presentation at *Recruitment International's* Gender Diversity Conference in London.

Perhaps the most inspiring element of her presentation - and her journey - is her life-long commitment to people and ethics. *"I am first and foremost a nurse and the ethos of delivering care and the highest quality of care is part of my essence as a person."*

"That sense of compassion and treating people with dignity remain cornerstones of how H1 Healthcare operates and will always be so."

Pam is truly an extraordinary person whose business will surely continue to go from strength to strength. ⌐

"THAT SENSE OF COMPASSION AND TREATING PEOPLE WITH DIGNITY REMAIN CORNERSTONES OF HOW H1 HEALTHCARE OPERATES AND WILL ALWAYS BE SO.

AUDENTES
FORTUNA JUVAT
COURAGE

C ourage is defined as the ability to act not in the absence of fear or doubt but in spite of it. All the leaders in this chapter have chosen a mindset and adopted a set of behaviours that have allowed them to act decisively when an opportunity appeared amidst the complex and sometimes bewildering forces that intervene in our business and personal lives.

However well-crafted our business plans might be they are subject always to a larger 'correlation of forces' (what during the Cold War the Russians called *sootnosheniye sil*) that can impact our business and personal lives in unexpected ways. These may be political, economic, social and cultural forces that change the way people view the world of work for example. They can be technological forces - such as the ubiquity of digital social media platforms over the past decade - that transform ways business has been conducted seemingly 'overnight'.

WHILST WE CANNOT CONTROL THESE FORCES WHAT WE CAN CONTROL IS OUR ATTITUDE TOWARD THEM AND THE BEHAVIOURS WE ADOPT WHEN CONSIDERING THESE FORCES."

Whilst we cannot control these forces what we can control is our attitude toward them and the behaviours we adopt when considering these forces. Those that do this consistently and successfully can sometimes appear to be blessed with disproportionate 'good luck' or good fortune. Researchers have however investigated this phenomenon of 'good luck' and discovered that it can be broken down into component behaviours that raise the odds of being 'lucky'.

Max Gunther in fact wrote a book called *The Luck Factor* in which he identified (after evaluating more than 1000 people) a number of particular actions/behaviours that so-called 'lucky' people tended to adopt. He discovered that a combination of some or all of these tended to position someone far better to cope with the inevitable changes that the larger 'correlation of forces' exerted in their lives.

They all contribute to the key trait of having courage which is encapsulated in the Latin phrase 'audentes fortuna juvat' meaning 'fortune favours the bold'.

Networking
One such behaviour adopted by 'lucky people' was developing a wide range of friendly contacts or what today we call 'networking'.

As Gunther says in his book: *"You cannot know what thunderbolt of good fortune is being prepared for you now by some distant engine of fate... But you can know with certainty... that the probability of your getting hit is directly proportional to the number of people who know your name."*

Matthew Eames' story in this chapter demonstrates this principle very well. Having spent his 'first career' working in the insurance markets of London he had developed a wide range of contacts and could not have known during these years that he was building an invaluable resource for his future recruitment career. And when the time came it was in part these connections that provided the foundation for him to soar so swiftly when he entered the world of recruitment in 1998; so much so that he increased his earnings by a factor of 10 within three years of leaving the world of insurance!

Similarly Andy Hogarth working diligently as a second hand car salesman impressed his bosses and their families; later a chance meeting with them lead to a conversation and his being backed to start his own business and his first foray into the world of recruitment via an Alfred Marks franchise.

Be Prepared

This aspect of courage is having a mindset that cultivates a sense of positive expectation; that is a sense of preparedness to act when the time is right. Adam Shulman was flourishing in the world of education recruitment (after initially being taken off the sales floor as he needed more training!) but had a sense of frustration working for someone else. He began to visualise and think about starting his own business even though no clear path was revealing itself. When a contact from a competitor called to invite him to become a partner in creating their own business he was ready and prepared to take the risk.

Grab Opportunities

It is also important to know the difference between boldness and rashness; when there is great uncertainty and fear it can be easy (and indeed be seen as rational and sensible) to delay a desire to start a new venture until market conditions are more propitious.

The 2008-2009 period was about as uncertain and fearful an economic climate one can imagine. Yet a 25 year old Charlie Walker decided to set up Vivid Resourcing and spent four months working alone cold calling before he could afford to hire and expand. Yet his inner conviction told him it was time to act and after finding backers took the leap in the worst economic recession for 80 years.

Similarly Dave Cook, with no recruitment experience at all, decided with brother Glenn (himself with 12 months in the sector), to create National Locums in 2009 working from their home and using a makeshift computer. Dave had several years' business experience and had reached a point where a new challenge was being sought but no clear idea of which sector this would arise within. But once Glenn had informed him of the growing opportunity within healthcare recruitment they grasped the nettle and have not looked back.

Have Faith

Analysis paralysis is something that successful leaders in recruitment do not suffer. Yes, they evaluate and collect information but insisting that you have all the information before you act means you will never leave the house!

'Lucky people' have the faith, once they have decided upon a course of action that inspires them, that what they do not know (and probably cannot know in advance) they will learn and adapt along the way. They back themselves to find a way.

Recent business research supports this notion. Eric Ries' 2011 book *The Lean Startup* has, according to some, radically altered the way we think about innovation and entrepreneurship. In essence Ries advocates converting ideas into products and services swiftly, bringing them into the market, then adapting the model as the market gives feedback.

Decades before *The Lean Startup* the inspirational Toni Cocozza was doing just this. Severely dyslexic, she left school with no qualifications aged 16, but thrived in the male-dominated world of IT recruitment. The welcomed importance given to gender diversity today was a distant dream back then; Toni for example had to endure the stress and strain of a negative reaction to her decision to start a family. This was one of the factors leading her to strike out on her own.

So without money, advisors or premises she set up DP Connect and backed herself to learn what she did not know about the intricacies of running a business along the journey; the rest is history. ∎

Key Points

▲ Be observant of the forces at work affecting
your business
▲ 'Luck' can be cultivated through mindset and behaviours
▲ People matter; network, network, network
▲ Be prepared and expect opportunity
▲ Be bold and don't over-analyse
▲ Get started; learn the rest along the way

TONI COCOZZA
MANAGING DIRECTOR
DP CONNECT

Toni Cocozza is the founder and MD of DP Connect the well-known and respected specialist IT recruiter. I had the privilege of sharing time with Toni at the bustling HQ of DP Connect in Bromley.

Today DP Connect is a business employing more than 50 people with a turnover in excess of £16 million, three offices and includes FTSE 100 companies such as BMW and Legal and General as clients. Toni's leadership has been recognised widely including her being highlighted in the prestigious Veuve Clicquot Business Woman of the Year Award, winner of the Ernst and Young Entrepreneur of the Year and numerous other recruitment industry awards. Given this and the fact she combines business with being

WHILST I WAS NOT TECH SAVVY I WAS GOOD WITH PEOPLE AND UNDERSTOOD INTUITIVELY THE NEED TO UNDERSTAND AND MEET CLIENT NEEDS."

parent to three girls aged 18-24 and could easily be a leading lady in any Fellini classic, it might appear that this success was inevitable.

Early Days in Recruitment

"Far from it. I left school with no qualifications and being severely dyslexic was certainly a challenge," Toni explained. *"I stumbled into recruitment at the age of 19 and worked with an IT recruitment business. Whilst I was not tech savvy I was good with people and understood intuitively the need to understand and meet client needs."*

In fact, her drive, ability to create commercially enriching relationships and deliver results over the next eight years saw her rise to the role of Sales Director. This was a great achievement in an environment which particularly at that time was overwhelmingly male.

Unfortunately, it was at this high point career-wise where gender did become significant.

Courage Amidst Challenges

"After eight years in recruitment I decided to start a family and this led to a total change in attitude toward me. Those were unenlightened times. There was no flexibility from my employers and coupled with the recessionary times (it was 1990) the company treated employees very harshly."

Appalled Toni took the courageous decision to set up DP Connect. *"I had no financial backing or overdraft and did not even have funds*

to pay the office rent. I reached an agreement to pay this in arrears from my first five deals!"

The rest, as they say is history. Toni's expertise has been recognised by her peers and she chaired the IT Division at the REC at a critical time for the sector as well as serving on APSCo's Executive Committee; she has also represented the recruitment industry as an advisor to the Government, acted as a business angel to recruitment start-ups and schemes including Young Enterprise, and instigated initiatives like Women in IT & IT Opportunities for All.

It has not been plain sailing of course; the recent recession brought many challenges to all recruiters.

"The period from 2008 has been the most challenging and we had to go back to the building blocks of business development. We supported our staff - which was crucial - and our ability to unite talent with technology, personally communicate with clients and develop bespoke, flexible solutions, meant we were pro-active in revenue generation"

Valuing People

I asked Toni, after nearly 25 years as an entrepreneur, what key lessons she had learned:

"My vision, from inception, was to create the business on the foundation that people come before profits - the clients, the candidates and our own people. That might not sound entrepreneurial but I know that by valuing all who work at DP Connect - whether through career progression or the ability to work flexibly -

we have been able to weather the inevitable economic ups and downs and provide continuity for our customers."

As a result, Toni has consultants who have been with her for 15-20 years and her first ever employee, taken on under the then Government YTS scheme, remains with DP! Furthermore, she has never had to seek outside investment for the business.

Indeed, DP Connect has expanded recently and opened new offices in Cambridge (2012) and Edinburgh (2013). This despite Toni having to face profound personal loss during this time:

"I lost my sister to cancer which happened with little warning. It was a devastating loss to me and my family and in part due to the loyalty and commitment of staff at DP the business has been able to develop even amidst these darkest of times."

Looking forward Toni is also looking at potential international expansion and her passion and drive are undimmed.

The word 'inspirational' is used far too frequently in today's instant gratification culture but it would be hard to find anyone more worthy of the accolade than Toni Cocozza.

"MY VISION, FROM INCEPTION, WAS TO CREATE THE BUSINESS ON THE FOUNDATION THAT PEOPLE COME BEFORE PROFITS.

06

CHARLIE WALKER
FORMER CEO - VIVID RESOURCING

Charlie Walker is the former CEO of Vivid Resourcing, the leading IT, energy and engineering recruitment business which he set up in 2008 aged 25(!!). It currently employs 52 people and places candidates in more than 50 countries and this year expects to exceed £30 million in turnover.

It is always a pleasure and a challenge to meet this fast and forward-thinking entrepreneur. He is just as at ease discussing a shared interest in political theory as he is the fortunes of his beloved Stockport County Football Club.

FRANKLY I NEEDED A NEW CHALLENGE AND MONEY HAS NEVER BEEN MY MAIN MOTIVATION."

I ask Walker about his early years and entry into recruitment. *"I was born in Stockport, brought up in Huddersfield and studied modern history and politics at Wadham College Oxford,"* he explains. Incidentally he also played in a drum and bass band (he graciously took time to explain this particular genre of music) with Riz Ahmed of 'Four Lions' and 'The Reluctant Fundamentalist' fame.

"I entered recruitment intending to stay for only 18 months. But I found that the meritocratic culture - age and background are extinguished as determinative factors - and the large element of competition matched perfectly with my personal goals."

Walker joined a recently-formed G2 Recruitment Solutions in Bristol and billed an astonishing £980,000 of GP within 24 months, achieving rapid promotion in the process. Despite this (and earning a handsome six-figure income) the then 25-year-old decided to set up his own business.

"Frankly I needed a new challenge and money has never been my main motivation. Offering a 'disruptive' model within recruitment appealed to me a lot. The reputation of the sector remains far from ideal due to the legacy of the 1990s era of juiced economic growth and a preponderance of overly aggressive sales types in the sector. Clients, I think, still associate that with the sector."

He found three experienced recruitment owners to back him and so in 2008 (*"the recession was beginning to unfold and there were some who mocked us starting the business from scratch at that point,"* he admits) Vivid was born.

06

He says, *"I worked alone for four months cold-calling all day - many of my established clients were not hiring due to the economic climate - and we then became profitable enough to hire a couple of graduates."*

The last seven years have seen stunning year-on-year growth. In 2013/14 the business grew 72% and Vivid is expected to exceed £30 million turnover this year. Much of this is attributable to the ethos Walker has created for the brand.

"I set up the business to change the perception of recruitment for all stakeholders including employees. Recruiters, within 12 months, typically see a 70-80% drop out from graduate trainees - a disgraceful waste of potential. Vivid has a 13-week training period and our attrition rate is 10%; exemplary for the sector. Building a team with true in-depth technical knowledge of their markets has been why we have so much repeat client business."

This has brought much recognition, including *Recruitment International's* 'Entrepreneur of the Year' award for Walker in 2014. Notwithstanding awards Walker is forthright about the need to continually innovate.

"We remain committed to the belief that clients value - and will pay attractive margins to - a recruitment business that can offer unrivalled depth of knowledge, speed of response and ability to secure the highest quality talent in key verticals."

Walker believes these factors ensure any 'threats' from the growth of in-house recruitment teams and RPO models is minimal:

Charlie Walker played in a drum & bass band while a student at Oxford.

he says, *"We focus on the niches where perhaps there are only 80-120 candidates skilled enough to do the relevant job. This is why we do not see threats from in-house teams that traditionally do not source these segments. We also have no truck with RPO offerings which not only deskill recruiters but are de facto facilitators of a destructive race to the bottom for our industry."*

Outside of work Walker is married and a proud father of his young daughter. He has a lifelong commitment to social justice (influenced by his parents - both teachers) and is a member of the Labour Party. He retains his love of music.

"Those who knew me in my teenage years and early twenties - I used to work in record shops and still love attending gigs - would probably find it amusing to see me wearing a city suit and running a business."

They may but, perhaps influenced by the teaching gene of his parents, Walker is at the forefront of educating the wider business world about the recruitment sector's commitment to ethics and professionalism.⌐

"I SET UP THE BUSINESS TO CHANGE THE PERCEPTION OF RECRUITMENT FOR ALL STAKEHOLDERS INCLUDING EMPLOYEES.

ADAM SHULMAN
CEO - SIMPLY EDUCATION

Adam is CEO of Simply Education, a fast-growing recruitment agency headquartered in Bedford with, as the name suggests, a specialisation in the education market. I met Adam at his HQ to learn about his remarkable story.

There was a palpable buzz when I entered Simply's cavernous offices and Adam updated me on the latest news about the company. Simply Education has some 54 employees and expects turnover for the current year to eclipse £10 million. 2014 was a year of milestones as new offices opened in Birmingham and Lincoln.

I BEGAN KNOCKING ON DOORS AND GOT MANY REJECTIONS - NO SALES EXPERIENCE - BUT FINALLY SECURED A ROLE AS A RECRUITMENT CONSULTANT."

"I left school at 16 and frankly stumbled into a job at McDonalds. A couple of years later I enrolled into college as had big dreams about education being a route to success but at age 19 my then girlfriend - now my wife and partner at Simply - and I had our daughter Kealie and it was really a question of working to provide for the family."

So he stuck with McDonalds for several years becoming an Assistant Manager in Dunstable, the town where Adam grew up in. But there remained within him a desire to secure economic success more rapidly than a conventional corporate career offered.

"I really knew virtually nothing about recruitment but I became convinced that it offered an opportunity. So I began knocking on doors and got many rejections - no sales experience - but finally secured a role as a recruitment consultant. This was with Teaching Personnel and it was 2002."

Was there a meteoric rise to sales stardom?

"Hardly! I found sales scary and after initial training I survived a few weeks on the sales floor before being asked to go back for some more training!"

Eventually he made it a success. Within a couple of years, he was asked by an investor to set up an education desk within the investor's existing business. Adam did this virtually single-handedly and rapidly was generating a six-figure GP. Within two years he decided that he could set up on his own and took what, in hindsight sounds like a huge risk:

"I had just enough money to put a deposit on a house - we were renting then - and calculated that I had enough money to pay the business's bills for two months so you could say there was a pressure to bill!"

Adam was soon joined by Sharon Sperrin - who had been a competitor - and they became business partners. Not long after, Adam's wife left her full-time job to join the business and Sharon's partner also joined. They remain the directors of the business to this day. They all have a firm commitment to being fair to employees and clients and Simply has built its reputation on its values and delivery.

Within two or so years the business was generating over £4 million in turnover and attracted the attention of external investors, one of whom Adam decided to partner with: *"This was really my business education; I quickly learned the key components of strategy and organisational development where the key is to admit your areas of weakness and hire talent that is better than you are. I also learned the basics of finance."*

After 4 years Adam felt he and the business had matured such that he parted ways with the investor which involved not a little contention, but eventually in November 2013 Adam and his three co-directors bought out the 25% stake the investor had been gifted literally 4 years previously.

Adam was pulled off the sales floor in his first month in recruitment as he was not performing well and needed more sales training!

"That episode is firmly behind us now and we have continued our upward growth trend this year. We have also invested resources in the business to add a vital international component to our business which we are confident will add to our success"

It should be noted that the secular trends within education recruitment remain encouraging. State-funded pupil numbers are forecast to grow from 6.2 million to around seven million in 2020. There is therefore a need for teachers that necessarily will grow to meet this demand.

Outside work Adam devotes his time to helping his daughter pursue her theatrical talents. Kealie is a pupil at the prestigious Italia Conti Academy of Theatre Arts in London. Adam is obviously proud of his daughter and there is an added poignancy to this particular story:

"When I was nine I auditioned for the Italia Conti Academy and was accepted but my parents could not afford for me to attend full time. Due to Simply Education and our great team I am privileged to allow my daughter to have the opportunity I could not."

As I said at the beginning a remarkable journey for Mr Shulman!

06

DAVID COOK
MANAGING DIRECTOR
NATIONAL LOCUMS

David Cook is the managing director of healthcare recruitment agency National Locums, based in Milton Keynes. Employing 40 people, the business specialises in the provision of medical locums and nursing professionals to more than 200 hospitals across the NHS and private sector.

Healthcare recruiters have had a torrid time of late, ranging from Health Secretary Jeremy Hunt accusing them of *"ripping off the NHS"* in June 2015, to the recent imposition of curbs on agency spend by the NHS. When one meets David Cook (or his co-founders, brother Glenn and their respective wives Jen and Natalie) and listens to his values

WE ALL USE THE NHS; IT IS SOMETHING OF WHICH WE CAN BE DEEPLY PROUD IN THIS COUNTRY."

about recruitment and the NHS it is impossible to associate him or National Locums with Hunt's diatribe. He says, *"We all use the NHS; it is something of which we can be deeply proud in this country. However, it cannot function without the vital contribution of locum doctors and nurses. National Locums has earned a reputation as a trusted partner to local hospitals across the UK."*

As well as the self-evident business case for developing trust relationships with the NHS there is a profound personal driver for Cook's beliefs. *"When my son Evan was born he was diagnosed with Bi-Coronal Craniosynostosis (early fusing of the skull). He has received wonderful treatment at the John Radcliffe Hospital in Oxford and had an successful operation in February 2015. Helping the healthcare system with their clinical workforce needs is much more than business for me."*

National Locums' commitment to corporate social responsibility, has included 25 of its employees scaling the heights of Ben Nevis (a challenge spearheaded by Natalie Cook) and raising significant sums for the local hospital children's ward.

National Locums has scaled its own heights since it was started in 2009 from the front room of a house by Cook and Glenn, Jen and Natalie. Its remarkable growth (evidenced by its move to fabulous new offices at the prestigious Manor Court Farm business centre at Old Wolverton, Milton Keynes) is particularly noteworthy given that Cook had no recruitment experience at all and Glenn about 12 months' worth!

Indeed, Cook's professional background has been far removed from recruitment. *"I am Milton Keynes born and bred and dropped out of sixth form as I had a passion for computers and left to study for a BTEC in Computer Studies; then worked within IT support for a national law firm for four years."*

Following this he moved to work with an IT distributor and while there was asked to upgrade the company website, and it was this opportunity that allowed his creative and commercial nous to flourish. He subsequently moved to Pauley Creative, a design company, to establish their web functionality. It was a pivotal moment for Cook as he explains, *"I was fortunate to be allowed significant autonomy to grow the web department and I learned an enormous amount about how to run a business from the managing director. He facilitated my passion to understand the nuances of successful management including the opportunity to attend Cranfield Business School."*

After more than six years Cook was at a point where a new challenge might be needed. And it was here that a confluence of circumstances led to the creation of National Locums. Cook recalls, *"I had always been aware of the opportunities within recruitment, and especially healthcare recruitment, through local friends as Milton Keynes has more than its fair share of such businesses. In addition, my brother Glenn who had spent a year within a medical recruitment business had mentioned the massive opportunity within the sector."*

So the team of four decided that the opportunity was too good to miss and began operating National Locums from home. They specialised only in locum psychiatrists at inception. Initially Cook continued working full time in his job and worked evenings applying the business management acumen he had gained to ensure the business was on a firm footing, even if the technology infrastructure was not state of the art. *"When we began I had a Tesco internet IP phone for our use but it kept cutting out! Our IT comprised a couple of old PCs I had knocking around but it was enough to get started!"* Cook says jokingly.

In fact, the business boomed and within three months Cook resigned from his job to work on building National Locums full time and apart from one episode in the very infancy of National Locums the business has never required additional investment capital as it has grown. Cook says, *"My management experience ingrained within me the importance of efficient processes and systems without which any business, however innovative, will struggle. This included a very tight control of cash flow which is particularly important when providing locums. Only once, right in the early days, I remember that I had to put an extra £200 into the business to ensure a locum received payment on time... it was enough to make sure we were world class in cash flow management!".*

In fact, National Locums' standards have been recognised repeatedly. It has earned a preferred supplier status on the GPS Framework and in 2014 won numerous additional Framework awards, including with Medway NHS Trust. Its turnover has grown from £2.4 million in year one to over £9 million for the year ended February 2015. Cook expects this to double to £18 million in 2016 as it expands its service offering.

"We took the strategic decision to start a nursing division in June 2014 and this has proved to be a key element in our confidence about future growth. The nursing division headcount doubled in six months and made a contribution of £900,000 in turnover. Our new office has capacity for 70 employees and we expect to hit those numbers rapidly."

Cook cites two important factors that have played key roles in National Locums' success, *"Our staff retention rates are very good within an industry and sector where staff turnover is notoriously high; when we began we made the commitment to live by being transparent and fair in how we treated our staff. Family values are everything for us."*

In addition, the business has developed a reputation by (literally in some cases) going the proverbial extra mile to help supply the talent needed by the hospitals it serves. *"The Noble Hospital on the Isle of Man is an important client and traditionally it has not been easy to source locums to work there due to the logistics of travel and the relative unfamiliarity of the island. So we sent our sales manager to the island for a few days to get an experiential insight which enabled us to not only source the clinicians needed but to help them seamlessly adjust to living and working on the Isle of Man."*

John Kotter, a Harvard Business School scholar, has emphasised that truly outstanding leaders need to have a clear vision in which their colleagues have belief and also be able to inspire them to continually make the changes needed to realise it. Cook and his co-founders exude these characteristics.

"The NHS is undergoing its most profound transformation since its formation. National Locums is proud to be partnering so many hospitals to provide the type of world class care all patients - including my son Evan who is scheduled to have another operation next year - need and deserve."

Vision, belief, inspiration...... Q.E.D. ⌐

"TRULY OUTSTANDING LEADERS NEED TO HAVE A CLEAR VISION IN WHICH THEIR COLLEAGUES HAVE BELIEF AND BE ABLE TO INSPIRE THEM TO CONTINUALLY MAKE THE CHANGES NEEDED TO REALISE IT.

MATTHEW EAMES
CEO - EAMES
CONSULTING

Matthew Eames is founder and CEO of Eames Consulting, an award winning recruitment and search firm which connects talent at the mid to senior level within the financial and professional services sectors. It currently has four offices around the world and more than 100 employees. It identifies and delivers talent from auditors to wealth managers, across specific market segments, ranging from insurance companies and investment banks to global consulting and advisory firms.

I met Eames on a glorious July afternoon and he was in a buoyant mood telling me, *"2014 was our best year as a business, we turned over £25 million and had 90 employees.*

IT IS IN OUR MOMENTS OF DECISION THAT OUR DESTINY IS SHAPED."

The first half of 2015 saw our NFI increase by 30% on prior year and we are likely to easily exceed £30 million in turnover"

I have been fortunate to spend time with Eames in recent months and one is struck by his focus and the clarity of vision for the business. The business has come a long way from a three-man startup in 2002. And all this after being rejected by a recruiter for "not being tenacious enough" when he first tried entering the sector: the irony abounds!

But we are running ahead of ourselves. Anthony Robbins, the world renowned performance coach and advisor to Presidents and celebrities, once said, *"It is in our moments of decision that our destiny is shaped".*

Arguably Eames's adult life has been marked by three critical (and courageous) decisions that have led him to where he is today.

The first was at university: *"I attended the University of the West of England and studied a financial services degree. Unfortunately, I failed a particular paper twice and was faced with the prospect of having to start the year again. I had however by then, had two stints of summer work at Lloyds of London and was keen to start a career, so I decided to leave academic life".* His tenacity had already been demonstrated as during university he would travel back to his parental home in Surrey and spend weekends washing cars and mowing lawns (which he had been doing from his early teens) to earn additional income. *"I wasn't afraid of hard work,"* as he puts it.

In addition to the hunger for hard work's rewards he had already developed a keen insight into the importance of networking: *"At the time, my girlfriend's father was a senior underwriter within the insurance market and I sent him my CV and asked him to circulate it. He called me the same day and offered me a job. I started the next day!"* This was 1993 and he began on the princely sum of £9,250 a year.

Over the next five years Eames gained exposure to different segments of the insurance market. It was then that he made the second momentous decision of his professional life: *"In 1998 I had elevated my earnings to £18,000 and received a bonus of £500 in 1998 after five years of hard work. I looked ahead and whilst the very long-term rewards to sticking to what I was doing were good, they were very long-term! I was frustrated to say the least".*

A close friend was working in the recruitment sector and advised Eames that he would be ideal for its fast paced environment. *"I stepped back and evaluated my strengths, which included building networks and working hard and frankly I'd had enough of being underpaid. I joined PSD and was promised that I would earn rewards commensurate with my effort. I was sold."*

He handed back his £500 bonus and focused on establishing PSD's technology and change management offering within the Lloyds market and, within two years, was its global top biller. His earnings in his third year were ten times his previous salary as an underwriter... fortune favours the bold!

Matthew was rejected for a role in recruitment as he was deemed "not tenacious enough!"

He now reached his third momentous career decision, to set up his own business, which he prosecuted with characteristic clarity:

"I told my then boss of my desire to set up on my own. She advised that having been in contract recruitment to date, I would need exposure to permanent and retained methodologies and kindly arranged for me to work within those sections of the business for the next 18 months. I also attended evening classes to learn the key elements of running a business".

'Strategy' is an oft-used (even misused) business school term. In essence it means the choices you decide to make to realise your vision and the way you will offer service in a differentiated way. In their 2013 book *Playing to Win*, Lafley and Martin identify the importance of defining how you will establish an advantage over your competition if your strategy has any chance of succeeding.

Eames seems to have done precisely that when he set up Eames Consulting Group in 2002: *"My motivation was not the financial returns. Having worked within the insurance market for almost a decade as underwriter and recruiter I focused on understanding what our customers valued and, importantly, how they wanted to be engaged with. From the start I wanted our offering to be defined by specific niches and delivered by consultants who were experts within them."*

In fact, the commitment to this vision remains at the heart of the business: *"Our core values are more than just words. Everyone across our global offices lives our commitment to be a trusted partner who is accountable, credible and equally importantly, ethical,"* Eames comments, highlighting the business's recent reiteration of its vision and values.

"We've also collected some industry awards and have been nominated one of the Best Companies to Work For several times". All this seemed a long way off back in 2002 when Eames Consulting Group began in a 500 square foot office in Hammersmith with a resourcer and administrator; Eames focused on his strength as a 'rain maker' and the business grew in the UK and internationally.

"We actually grew during the global financial crisis. Our strategy of focusing on the insurance market has enabled us to build a global business, following our clients and establishing offices in Singapore in 2010, Switzerland in 2012 and Hong Kong in 2014. I was comfortable dealing with international cultures and saw so much opportunity having travelled so much as a child, as my father was a pilot for more than 30 years," Eames explains.

"We've got plans to grow the existing business and enter new geographies and are always looking for talented, like-minded individuals to join us".

A key part of Eames's growth as a leader has been to strengthen his leadership team and constantly develop its offering. *"Being an entrepreneur can be lonely and in 2006 I invited Chris Herrmannsen (formerly CEO of TMP and Ochre House) to join the board as non-executive director and his experience has been invaluable. In addition, late last year, Guy Day joined us as global COO; he has lived in Asia for 18 years and previously led the Ambition business."*

Outside the everyday bustle of his business Eames has a busy home life with his wife, Caroline, and their three children (two boys and a girl) and he admits to a love of wine *("not only as a consumer but I also invest in wine")* and being a dab hand at cooking!

Interestingly Eames's passion for business has expanded and for the last five years he has been an investor and board member of Brightsparks Recruitment Ltd, which helps students and graduates find temporary work whilst at University and also permanent positions after completing their studies.

"OUR CORE VALUES ARE MORE THAN JUST WORDS. EVERYONE ACROSS OUR GLOBAL OFFICES LIVES OUR COMMITMENT TO BE A TRUSTED PARTNER WHO IS ACCOUNTABLE, CREDIBLE AND EQUALLY IMPORTANTLY, ETHICAL.

06

ANDY HOGARTH
CEO - STAFFLINE

Andy Hogarth is the CEO of Stock Exchange listed Staffline, which provides temporary staff to sectors including industrial, manufacturing and logistics and also services in the welfare to work arena.

I met Andy on the top floor of the Gherkin in London and enjoyed a glorious vista over the square mile; symbolically apt given that Staffline, during 2014, had seen its share price rise from 555p to 895p and even touched 1000p in July of that year! By the end of 2014 the company had a market cap of over £225 million. Andy is a qualified accountant and an impressively articulate and highly successful leader of a listed business.

I LEFT SCHOOL AT 16 WITH FEW QUALIFICATIONS AND DID A NUMBER OF VARIED JOBS - A CAREER IT WAS NOT."

His has been an extraordinary journey. *"Actually I left school at 16 with few qualifications and did a number of varied jobs - a career it was not - for a number of years before becoming a second hand car salesman in north London,"* Andy explains. Meeting Andy today, it taxes the imagination to see him selling motors in a sheepskin coat! Being unfulfilled he left car sales and then 'Lady Fortune' intervened. Andy recalls, *"The car of one of the owner's wives of one of the car businesses I had previously worked for had broken down on the North Circular road and I bumped into her; cutting a long story short she said they had faith in me and would back me in a business venture."*

Andy acquired an Alfred Marks franchise in 1987 and after a struggle in his first year with the business, used his drive and ambition to make it into one of the highest billing franchises in the network. He sold it after three years, but despite having money in the bank and a sense of commercial achievement he became depressed. *"I had no plan about what to do next. I lost a year of my life and felt a profound loss of identity and purpose. It was a very challenging year indeed."*

He then took the courageous decision to re-train as an accountant going to work for the firm that had helped him sell the franchise and in his thirties went back to university to get qualified. Not only did he do that, he also met his wife, Helena, in the process! He joined another firm of accountants and in 1994 was asked to step

06

in as 'interim finance director' at Pipeline Constructors Group, a business specialising in the outsourcing of water, gas and electricity construction for all the utility companies.

Andy says, *"The business was in financial trouble and was losing control of its overdraft. I realised it was really a cash flow management issue and I enjoyed driving the financial turnaround. Within a year an overdraft of over two million was paid off."* Andy's business and professional acumen recognised a business with upside potential and he led the MBO as finance director. He stayed until 2002 when it was sold and by which time it had turnover of £100 million and delivering EBIT of £3 million.

He says, *"This time I ensured I had another project and I joined Staffline as a finance director in August 2002. There were a number of issues, however, and the business was feeling the weight of debt."* It was a deja vu experience as Andy took leadership of managing the finances.

He eventually became managing director and during his time with the company, Staffline has undergone staggering growth. It listed on AIM in 2004 and currently has more than £500 million turnover, operates from 300 locations and provides more than 43 million hours of temporary labour each year. *"Our core business remains recruitment and we service more than 1,300 clients. Through acquisition and contract wins our welfare to work business is also growing rapidly."* Andy emphasises. *"We have built the business on an ethical foundation and are proud to be the only organisation with representation on the boards of REC, ALP and GLA."* Outside of Staffline, Andy owns Hogarths, a boutique hotel in salubrious

Andy is a qualified accountant and owns Hogarths, a boutique hotel.

Solihull and has previously owned a nursing home for more than 20 years.

Andy's extraordinary journey is testimony to his desire for self-improvement and an example of how people can make the most of the opportunities for business development available in the UK. This ordinarily would be an apposite point to conclude this feature but I must mention one other event in Andy's life that puts all of the above in perspective. Andy and Helena became immensely proud parents in 2013, their son Toby is without doubt the apple of Andy's eye. So as well as running a £200 million+ market cap business, being a hotelier and qualified accountant, he is also adept at changing nappies... and who says men cannot multitask!

"WE HAVE BUILT THE BUSINESS ON AN ETHICAL FOUNDATION AND ARE PROUD TO BE THE ONLY ORGANISATION WITH REPRESENTATION ON THE BOARDS OF REC, ALP AND GLA.

07

INFLECTION POINTS
FORTITUDE

The world of business has been subject to profound change over the past two or three decades and that change is happening at a rate that is itself increasing. Naturally enough the recruitment sector in many ways is unrecognisable from the industry it was in the 1980s or 1990s.

Digitisation, globalisation, new technologies and demographic change (including the need to recognise diversity) are just a few of the mega trends that impact the recruitment sector.

Andy Grove, the former CEO of Intel, in his 1996 book *Only the Paranoid Survive,* uses the term 'inflection point' to describe periods when profound change occurs and which if ignored can lead to the extinction of a business or even an industry. Think of the transition from cassettes to CD's and the 'Big Bang' in the City of London in the latter half of the 1980's.

In Grove's words: *"Strategic Inflection Points are about fundamental change in any business, technological or not."* And yet despite the enormity of these Inflection Points they can sometimes seem to have occurred almost imperceptibly.

"Most Strategic Inflection Points, instead of coming with a bang, approach on little cat feet. They are often not clear until you can look at the events in retrospect," Grove argues.

The recruitment leaders featured in this chapter have lived through more than one inflection point given their vast experience: Richard Herring, John Hailstone, Karen Silk and Steve Ingham all began their recruitment careers in the 1980s and all after a period in another industry.

The sector has moved from print-based job advertisements to websites and now job boards and social media based platforms that seek to directly match candidate to client. The global nature of the search for talent has also been a key transformation as has the rise in complexity in terms of regulatory and legislative intervention in the sector.

It is interesting to note how the leaders featured here have positioned their businesses and undertaken the necessary change or transformation to ensure continued success amidst these trends.

Albert Ellis (who began working life as a jazz musician in South Africa before training as an accountant) was able to draw on his financial and wide business acumen to ensure that Harvey Nash was shoring up its finances in the period leading up to the global financial crisis of 2008; itself an inflection point whose macro-economic impact remains felt to this day.

Elsewhere Richard Herring and John Hailstone deliberately undertook a strategy of diversification as part of their plan to work within the increasing globalisation of world markets. Richard joined Volt in 2005 and executed the remit to expand in international markets which contributed to the business being able to ride the tidal wave of market uncertainty after Lehman. John anticipated ever increasing reliance on in-house recruitment teams amongst clients and, in addition to international expansion committed Compello Group to offer specialist expertise in key verticals. His equity participation model for those who lead the various Group businesses was also designed to ensure that the best talent was retained.

Whilst inflection points are not necessarily driven by technological change, the rapid proliferation of the digital economy has acted as an agent of dramatic disruption in business models across all sectors from retail to banking. Michelle Watson, after 20 successful years within Accountancy and Finance recruitment, left Page Group's executive Board and later joined Gemini which has expertise in the creative digital world. She has literally made the inflection point her friend in her career!

If strategic inflection points are sometimes hard to properly appreciate until after the fact how can one prepare for their impact? Andy Grove is candid in *Only the Paranoid Survive*:

"The only way is through the process of clarification that comes from broad and intensive debate."

Jason Stewart and DRC Locums are eloquent advocates in exactly such a debate currently dominating the healthcare recruitment sector. Government demonisation and repressive policies such as agency spend and rate caps have been imposed on a sector itself starved of funding to train the very medical professionals needed to meet patient need. DRC has thrived by offering outstanding and flexible service delivery models and best in class compliance with the dynamics of a healthcare sector in a state of flux.

And it's not just specific sectors that face ever greater change and competition to capture the value created in a market. It is simply a fact of business life. As Andy Grove pointedly put it:

"Business success contains the seeds of its own destruction. The more successful you are, the more people want a chunk of your business and then another chunk and then another."

And as one surveys the last three decades Steve Ingham and Karen Silk respectively have not just survived but thrived in such a climate for the world of recruitment has certainly not become any less competitive.

Page remains a world class recruitment brand across many verticals and Capital International a respected and trusted expert provider in niche engineering sectors. Both leaders in their very different ways have created business models that have not only endured but which have inculcated great loyalty and longevity amongst their teams.

Things to remember:

▲ Keep learning about the economy both local and global
▲ Embrace change for it will inevitably embrace you!
▲ Constantly question your model to find ways to improve all aspects of it
▲ Encourage debate and critique from within to achieve this improvement
▲ Have a culture that delivers stable and aligned teams

ALBERT ELLIS
CEO - HARVEY NASH

This year Albert Ellis will have served 10 years as CEO of Harvey Nash, the global provider of talent (across executive search, professional recruitment and outsourcing) which has 7,700 consultants and IT professionals across 43 countries. It has a market capitalisation of approximately £60 million and employs more than 800 consultants and recruiters.

Intriguingly recruitment is his third profession in a working life spanning both hemispheres and almost 40 years. *"I was born in South Africa and from a young age had a passion for and enough talent as a musician to pursue this professionally from age 14,"* Ellis explains, recalling a South Africa much different from today.

THE PERIOD 1998-2005 WAS EXCITING, BUT I ALSO WITNESSED FIRST-HAND THE DOT-COM BUBBLE BURSTING AND THE IMPACT OF 9/11 ON THE US ECONOMY."

"Apartheid was a fact of life at that time. It affected all communities. I still recall, as a child, hearing my father, who was an electrical engineer within the telecom sector, saying that his career prospects were stifled due to his being English rather than an Afrikaner." Ellis continued for some years as a musician but realised that he would not be able to reach the top tier where it was possible to earn a living. Ellis's uncle (a successful entrepreneur) was a mentor at this important crossroads.

He advised Ellis to qualify as a chartered accountant, if he wanted a successful career in business. *"I undertook full time study attending evening and weekend lectures at the Wits University in Johannesburg, while still working full time including a manual job in a store in a Government department!"* he recalls. He qualified as an accountant in 1992. By then he had met and married his wife (who is English and was travelling in South Africa) and they relocated to the UK in 1993. Ellis elaborates, *"My love of music meant I wanted to work for EMI but I was unsuccessful and I was offered a senior role with FTSE 100 Hays plcs recruitment division and frankly I knew nothing about recruitment as a sector.*

After two years, I transferred to its logistics division which supplied to leading UK retailers and it was fascinating." He joined Harvey Nash in 1998 and his years as CFO were certainly interesting: *"The period*

1998-2005 was exciting, but I also witnessed first-hand the dot-com bubble bursting and the impact of 9/11 on the US economy, when we lost a whole month of sales as a result."

Ellis was promoted to CEO in 2005 and now, 10 years later, the business has extended its footprint globally (including its August 2014 acquisition of Beaumont KK, an executive search firm in Japan) and has revenues in excess of £700 million. Harvey Nash also has no long term debt and perhaps reflects Albert's financial rigour borne of being an accountant: He says, *"Quite a few FTSE business CEOs have an accounting background. Business has become increasingly complex, and financial literacy is an advantage to any executive running a global business today. Over the years I have tried to apply some of the timeless wisdom of 'value investing' to Harvey Nash as enunciated by Warren Buffet's teacher Benjamin Graham in the 'Intelligent Investor', my favourite book."*

Ellis is proud that Harvey Nash is playing a critical role in the professionalisation of the recruitment sector: *"As we have spread our reach across the globe, whether it is placing senior executive talent or helping with BPO services through our Vietnam operations, we have developed our own talent in-house to ensure we have true experts in each niche market. We now recruit from leading universities in the USA, UK and Sweden."* Outside of work, Ellis is kept busy with his two teenage children and keeps fit through cycling.

His international experience has made him an advocate of the European project, however he clarifies, *"This does not mean I agree with all political initiatives coming out of Brussels; but I do believe*

Albert Ellis began life as a jazz musician at the age of 14, in South Africa.

in the idea that free movement within European markets will bring not only economic benefits but greater co-operation and ongoing understanding amongst cultures."

The importance of cultural acuity is seen in two important initiatives from Harvey Nash close to Ellis's heart: *"I have not forgotten the impact cultural and race barriers had in South Africa including to my father's career ambitions. I am proud therefore of 'Inspire', launched in 2008, to tackle under-representation of women on corporate boards and which now has more than 5,000 members internationally. In January this year we launched 'Engage' to offer a platform for people from diverse cultural backgrounds (similarly under-represented) to network and offer peer to peer support."* he explains.

He adds, *"It can be easy to marginalise those from backgrounds we do not understand or which are different but I believe we have a duty to facilitate the flowering of talent irrespective of background."*

Amen to that.

"FINANCIAL LITERACY IS AN ADVANTAGE TO ANY EXECUTIVE RUNNING A GLOBAL BUSINESS TODAY.

RICHARD HERRING
MANAGING DIRECTOR
VOLT

Richard is managing director for Europe and Asia at Volt, the US provider of talent with a global reach. Over 26 years within recruitment has made him a well-known and respected leader and in 2014 he was elected to the APSCo Board for the third time. Interestingly Richard's working life encompasses a couple of other sectors prior to his entry into recruitment.

"I grew up in Surrey and left school at 16. I cannot say I was the most academic schoolboy but the hotel and catering industry appealed so I started a course in hotel management. After the first year I accepted that I just didn't want to study and left the course to find a job."

WORKING LIFE SUITED ME AND I MADE MY WAY UP THE RANKS AND BECAME ONE OF THE YOUNGEST DEPARTMENT MANAGERS IN THE COMPANY."

Richard started a job in retail, working for Debenhams. He recalls, *"I began as a temporary shelf filler, once even standing in as Santa! Working life suited me and I made my way up the ranks and became one of the youngest department managers in the company at the time. I also enjoyed surfing with many trips to Cornwall, Devon, Wales and the South West of France".* Baywatch eat your heart out!

He became restless however and took the bold step of completely changing commercial sectors. Attracted by the excitement and economic potential of the City, he entered the world of financial services sales. *"This was a very sales-driven culture with cold calling the foundation of business development. It was a challenge, very different from the relatively reactive retail sales model, and this honed my skills for the move into recruitment."*

This happened in 1988 when he joined Reed Computing in Guildford. *"There was a combination of entrepreneurial ethos and structure that helped me thrive. I was quickly promoted, becoming one of the top three billers within Reed as a consultant and by 1999 was appointed operations director."*

During the next five years, under Richard's leadership, the business quadrupled its turnover. After 16 years with Reed, Richard left to do

07

something different and joined The Skillsmarket, which was offering innovative digital CV facilities for candidates. The lure of recruitment, however, was too powerful and he was headhunted in 2005 to join Volt as its director of European Staffing Services. Richard says, *"The move to Volt was something I relished. I had the opportunity to drive the growth of the business across a number of countries in Europe. Recruitment may appear simple, at its essence it is; but traversing the complex commercial issues that arise from varying cultural and regulatory regimes is anything but simple!"*

Richard travelled extensively and unsocial hours - visits to Heathrow/ Gatwick were compensated by 'having' to visit the Volt office in the Cote d'Azur! In 2010 Richard was appointed managing director for Europe and Asia amidst the financial crisis which was in full flow following Lehman's implosion in late 2008. *"Fortunately we had begun to diversify beyond IT & Telecoms into other areas including engineering and Life Sciences. This diversification, alongside our geographical spread, helped us deal with the financial crisis with minimum impact."*

Richard has long been a champion of the recruitment sector and for the continual need to execute ever higher levels of service (he is a Six Sigma specialist) based on strong ethical foundations. His three stints at APSCo are firmly part of this vision: *"I am privileged to have been elected a third time to serve on the APSCo Committee. I believe APSCo's work is vital in developing amongst all stakeholders, including the Government, a deeper understanding and appreciation of our sector's worthiness and the value it provides to the economy."*

At a time of considerable scrutiny of the sector Richard's words could hardly be more apposite. Outside work Richard now skis rather than surfs and is a lifelong Spurs fan (a subject he did not want to elaborate upon!). He is also kept firmly on his toes by two teenage daughters; literally when he joined them at the recent Capital Radio Jingletime Ball!

Having worked through at least three recessions during his quarter century in recruitment I asked him if he had any advice to those commencing a career in the sector:

"Given technological and wider economic trends it is difficult to see recruiters being required to do anything other than enhance their services whilst managing costs carefully. However, this business is fundamentally predicated on understanding the needs of people and that cannot substantively be done by a machine. So, provided you do your job properly and always strive to add value to your clients and candidates you will thrive. It is a fantastic career choice."

"THIS BUSINESS IS FUNDAMENTALLY PREDICATED ON UNDERSTANDING THE NEEDS OF PEOPLE AND THAT CANNOT SUBSTANTIVELY BE DONE BY A MACHINE

MICHELLE WATSON
CEO - GEMINI
PEOPLE

Michelle Watson is the CEO of Gemini People, a leading agency for the creative, permanent and freelance markets. Launched in 2011, rapid growth has seen the company expand from three people to 60 and earned it awards including MARA's Best Newcomer and 8th place in the Sunday Times 100 Best Small Companies to Work For 2015.

Watson's career can best be described as living by being true to oneself, courageous and taking the proverbial road less travelled.

It is November 2008. Lehman Brothers has fallen and markets are plummeting. That month Watson is invited to join the UK Board of Michael Page (PageGroup), the

MY DRIVE COMES FROM BEING BORN INTO A WORKING CLASS IRISH FAMILY, BASED IN BIRMINGHAM, AND HAVING BEEN ENCOURAGED FROM AN EARLY AGE TO DEVELOP A HUNGER TO SUCCEED."

culmination of a 12-year career that she began as a consultant. Yet less than two years later she resigned, with no clear idea of her next career step.

This, however, was not the first time she had taken a leap into the unknown. *"I am a survivor and I am driven,"* she explains as we meet at Gemini's offices in the West End. *"My drive comes from being born into a working class Irish family, based in Birmingham, and having been encouraged from an early age to develop a hunger to succeed."*

A furious work ethic was evident at a young age, when she decided to get a job after completing her A-levels, rather than going to university. *"Since the age of 15 I sometimes worked 20 hours a week in my spare time. I did not want to be an impoverished student,"* Watson recalls.

Following her decision, she says, *"My mum insisted that I get a 'trade' and after replying to an advert for a trainee accountant with the local bus company my career path began!"*

She spent nearly the whole of the next decade as an accountant (later working for Cable and Wireless) and during this period, aged 21, she bought her first home, although that wasn't without its

07

difficulties. *"Around that time interest rates hiked to 14%, but I just about managed to make the mortgage payments!"*

In 1995, Watson decided that she was *"seriously bored with accountancy"* but had no idea what she would do instead. So she met with Michael Page as a potential candidate to see if they could help with her next career move. Seven interviews later, over a period of three months, they managed to convince her to join them! Watson says, *"The tipping point was when they showed me the company car list - which featured an MX5 - I signed up that day!"*

So was this driven, focused professional an instant success? Not quite. *"The first year was really tough,"* Watson tells me. *"I remember crying a lot! But I had a good manager, the hunger to do the cold calls and work the long hours - 8.30 am to 8.30 pm - with a 6 pm finish on Friday, and so I flourished."*

She had to face a fair few challenges. *"I was focused on permanent recruitment in the accounting/finance space, working with SME businesses in the Black Country in the West Midlands,"* she says. *"I met more than my fair share of sexism. It was thought natural by some that not only would accountants be men, but that a male recruiter would find them!"*

Over time, Watson's leadership skills were recognised and a number of management promotions followed, though it was not plain sailing, Watson admits. *"My first management role involved inheriting a team of five, all of whom promptly left! Eventually I understood the critical importance of hiring like-minded people, with common values as key*

EVENTUALLY I UNDERSTOOD THE CRITICAL IMPORTANCE OF HIRING LIKE-MINDED PEOPLE, WITH COMMON VALUES AS KEY TO SUCCESSFUL TEAM BUILDING."

to successful team building. By my third year in management I had the fastest growing finance recruitment team in the UK."

Later, during the 2000-03 recession, she set up the Page Personnel brand in the Midlands. This grew rapidly, with five new offices opening in two years. Eventually, this led to Watson's appointment to the Board of Michael Page and she was rightly proud to have broken the glass ceiling as a female recruitment professional. In 2010, however, after 15 years with Michael Page, she decided she wanted a change of direction, explaining, *"I just believe life is too short - I admit I was terrified to walk away from corporate life - yet I also felt a sense of liberation."*

Over the next couple of years Watson and husband Gary (whom she met at Michael Page) decided to start a family and son Archie arrived in 2011. By this time, she was also being approached by people seeking her considerable commercial experience of recruitment. *"An ex-employee invited me to advise on a new online recruitment solution - www.thejobpost.co.uk. It was lots of fun. I found it inspiring and invigorating to be working with entrepreneurial people; it was far away from the corporate world I had known. In fact, I did not expect to work directly in a recruitment business again."*

_07_

She then met James Caan which led to Watson meeting the founders of Gemini and rediscovering her enthusiasm for recruitment. She joined as managing director in 2012, and recalls, *"I was inspired by the vision for the business and also saw that the markets Gemini was focusing on offered incredible growth opportunities. But above all I felt that I had found kindred spirits in that the values of the business chimed so deeply. Gemini doesn't simply place people, we pair like-minded people whose talent and attitudes both complement and enrich."*

Watson helped Gemini in its organisational development and structure and this year was promoted to CEO, while leading the business in its rebrand. It has grown rapidly during her tenure, and like her team she lives the values of taking responsibility, believing in people and also ensuring that innovation and growth are based on honesty and transparency. She says, *"We consciously instil a work together, play together and high performance culture and we believe this ultimately results in happy and fulfilled people."*

There is also a clear and ambitious plan, as Watson reveals, *"We aim to secure an MBO on our terms in the next 18 months by 2018 and by 2020 open our first international office."*

As Watson reflects on 20 years within recruitment, across two very different businesses, she speaks with refreshing candour about the sector. *"Recruitment is not easy. I remember my first year vividly. I am honest enough to tell newcomers that the rewards are great - but don't enter with rose tinted glasses. You will have some tough times especially early on and at times you may hate it!"*

Her passion for the sector, however, is clear. *"I envisage this will be my last role in recruitment. It is a privilege as, having climbed the corporate ladder, I now have the opportunity to help others realise their true potential. I am honestly having the best fun I have had in 20 years in the industry."* ⌐

"GEMINI DOESN'T SIMPLY PLACE PEOPLE, WE PAIR LIKE-MINDED PEOPLE WHOSE TALENT AND ATTITUDES BOTH COMPLEMENT AND ENRICH.

JOHN HAILSTONE
CEO - COMPELLO STAFFING GROUP

John Hailstone is chairman of Compello Staffing Group, which invests in and manages specialist staffing businesses, including business and recruitment outsource services. Operating across many sectors of the global employment market including aviation, engineering, energy, financial services, business consulting, information technology, professional services and healthcare, the Group has a turnover of circa £70 million, with NFI of circa £12 million and employs 160 staff.

The late Muhammad Ali often said that a champion is made of a combination of will and skill driven by a burning desire. If this is so, then Hailstone has displayed a champion's will

I WORKED EVENINGS AND WEEKENDS EARNING ABOUT £100 PER WEEK - THIS WAS IN 1982! IT WAS A BRILLIANT EXPERIENCE WHICH TAUGHT ME SKILLS YOU COULDN'T PICK UP AT SCHOOL."

throughout his inspirational journey. Hailstone recalls, *"My parents separated when I was five. I remember it being a very difficult time. The social services asked my two older siblings where we wanted to live – they chose London and my very strict father. I didn't see my mother again until I was 23."*

A Tough Childhood Helped His Business Resolve

This experience has informed his commercial life: *"This experience of abandonment, I believe helped shape my resolve. It probably made me strong and resolute to my own cause,"* he says. *"I think this is a characteristic of most entrepreneurs."*

This resolve was channelled into a desire for success early on: *"I've had many jobs from the age of nine but at 15 I secured telesales work for Auto Trader. I worked evenings and weekends earning about £100 per week - this was in 1982! It was a brilliant experience which taught me skills you couldn't pick up at school."*

Inevitably school took a back seat and Hailstone left with no formal qualifications. However, his telesales experience helped secure a role as a trainee marine insurance broker in the city. His drive and commercial experience meant he rapidly excelled and he has vivid memories of those days. *"The city was gritty, exciting and going through dramatic changes. I also remember it being a very*

intimidating environment; quill pens, broad pinstripe suits and Church's brogues." Despite being told he was the youngest broker with a portfolio in Lloyds of London's history, he quit after two years to move to Glasgow for a girl he met through a friend. Whilst ultimately that romance did not work out, Hailstone has no regrets:
"I moved because it seemed like a big adventure. I didn't want to look back and wonder what life might have been."

So in October 1986, from a bedsit in Glasgow, Hailstone joined the world of recruitment at a national agency. His talent was recognised and within three months he was invited to join a start-up (which became Midas Recruitment Group) and learned the art of a 360-degree recruiter in a world where clients preferred using press adverts rather than an agency. He tells me, *"My manager was a real disciplinarian and taught me that success was gained through high activities, early starts and strong KPIs. The market was also still in its infancy so it meant vacancies were hard to come by but that taught me the skills to be a success, i.e. building strong relationships with both candidates and clients."*

Setting Up Independently

After three years Hailstone decided, aged just 23, it was time to take the risk of creating his own business and with a friend (John Farmer) set up Mackenzie Munro. Within six months, however, tragedy struck when his friend died of a heart attack yards from the office. Worst of all he had to formally identify him and then keep the business going. *"I'd lost my good friend - it was a very stressful time but I had to dig deep,"* he says. *"I carried on for another six months but realised I was doing it for the wrong reasons and John's death would always hang over the business which I didn't want."*

THE OWNERS NEEDED SOMEONE TO HELP THEM GROW THEIR FOUR-PEOPLE BUSINESS. I DIDN'T MIND GIVING UP 50% OF MY BILLINGS FOR THE CHANCE TO BE INVOLVED IN SOMETHING AGAIN!

He was invited to join KFJ recruitment on a self-employed basis amidst the 1991 recession. *"The owners needed someone to help them grow their four-people business. I didn't mind giving up 50% of my billings for the chance to be involved in something again!"* Hailstone was eventually promoted to director, promised a stake in the business and built it to 50 recruiters across Scotland. But before shares were given the business was sold and rather than fight the share promise he used the opportunity to start his own business again at aged 31.

He reveals, *"I sold my house and used all my savings to take a business plan to the bank so I could raise enough money to get First People Solutions started in 1998. Scale was important as it would lay the foundations for later success."*

After 12 years in recruitment he had a clear vision for the technology and engineering specialist: *"I set up FPSG to be a total solutions provider and to focus on its people. I believed this would provide the best growth as opportunities in Scotland, being a niche company, were very restrictive."* After initially setting up divisions providing both permanent, contract and temporary services across Sales, IT and Construction, other markets followed such as financial services, aviation, banking and others.

Due Recognition

Within 8 years John had created a sizeable business with offices across the UK, 100 staff and had completed two multi million pound acquisitions. Recognition followed including numerous Scottish Recruitment Awards, two Sunday Times Fast Track Awards and an Institute of Directors - Director of the Year Award.

Then the global financial crisis struck. *"I had been through a number of recessions before but nothing as bad as this. We had to cut costs and closed branches to survive."*

Anticipating that clients would move to in-house recruiting, he drew on his experience to re-orientate his business with three important decisions:
- To specialise in order to secure higher margins and differentiate
- To grow overseas presence in undeveloped recruitment markets to diversify
- To create a group model that rewarded valuable leaders in the business.

"This is where I thought up the idea for Compello Staffing Group and our management equity modelled structure," says Hailstone.

An International Platform Today

Compello Staffing Group, still headquartered in Glasgow, operates six recruitment businesses (including two sub brands), offices throughout Scotland, two in London and international offices in Qatar, Dubai, America (Houston, San Francisco and Boston) and Kurdistan; each is supported by a back office company. Hailstone

I HAVE A VIEW THAT WITH EVERY PROBLEM OR CHALLENGE COMES AN OPPORTUNITY."

explains, *"I act as mentor/advisor, helping the boards formulate the right strategies for success or in some cases knowing how to deal with adversity such as the down turn in the oil and gas market. I have a view that with every problem or challenge comes an opportunity."*

When the price of oil began to drop, Hailstone decided to support the existing oil and gas business rather than lose talented staff and saw the exceptional opportunities in the US and Middle East market.

He acted boldly to acquire a Middle East recruiter, reorganised the existing business as he integrated it and diversified into the chemicals and pharma industries. Following Hailstone's intervention, the business is back on track and much more balanced with only 20% of revenue now coming from the UK oil and gas market.

Compello Group is thriving and its overseas focus has resulted in it being ranked 109th in this year's Sunday Times HSBC International Track 200, Britain's fastest growing private companies for overseas sales. Outside of work Hailstone and wife Caroline are proud parents to two daughters (both aged under 10). He is also a golf fanatic, which he took up aged 40 and with typical determination is getting closer to his goal of shooting single figures before he turns 50! Muhammad Ali also used to say that without risk-taking, one would accomplish nothing in life. There can be little doubt that Hailstone has had the courage to take risks during his 30-year journey that makes him a champion of which the recruitment sector can be proud.

KAREN SILK
CEO - CAPITAL INTERNATIONAL STAFFING

Karen Silk is CEO at Capital International Staffing, which specialises in engineering recruitment throughout the UK and Europe. Based in Burgess Hill in Sussex, it has been established for over 30 years and specialises in the aerospace, automotive, defence, and telecoms sectors. The business employs 20 people and has a turnover of £7 million.

Passion (for business and life) is a word that always comes to mind when I share time with Silk. Anyone who was present at the *Recruitment International* Gender Diversity in Recruitment Conference in 2014 will recall

THE UK IS FACING A CRITICAL SHORTAGE OF ENGINEERS AND THIS WILL IMPACT OUR ABILITY TO COMPETE IN THE GLOBAL MARKET."

her inspirational address; *"I am deeply committed to encouraging young people, and especially girls, who have an aptitude and interest in physics and mathematics at GCSE to consider a career in engineering. The UK is facing a critical shortage of engineers and this will impact our ability to compete in the global market."*

2014 was also the year that Silk became a member of the APSCo Representative Committee. Her experience within engineering recruitment (and prior to that in the highly technical world of scientific instruments) has contributed to Capital becoming such a well-respected brand with global businesses in its key verticals.

It seems a long way from Silk's country roots, although her formative years laid the seeds of her entrepreneurial spirit. She says, *"I grew up in Cambridge and my parents were commercial farmers. My family had roots in farming going back to 1824. I remain a country girl at heart and have had a lifelong affinity to it. Hard work and drive were built into me from childhood and I recall waking at dawn and driving tractors at age 13! With my family role models, I guess I simply assumed that I would eventually end up working for myself."*

Armed with this strong work ethic, Silk completed a one-year business course at Anglia Ruskin University after her A-levels and as part of the course she made a presentation to a local Cambridge business's HR director and was invited to join them. The business specialised in the manufacturing of spectrophotometry and gas chromatography equipment and was eventually acquired by Phillips. Silk flourished during her nearly seven years there:

"I thrived in the world of business and was given experience across all the parts of the business. This included the sales function, where I specialised in the East European and Russian markets. I worked closely with research and was then given a senior role in finance. I also sat on the executive committee (with responsibility for all of Europe), which instilled the critical importance of financial control. Phillips's world class training enabled me to have the all-round experience to run my own business!"

Her opportunity to do this came, as it so often does, in a rather unexpected way. It was late 1984 and by then Silk had met her husband (Graham) while he was working for another division of Phillips as a software engineer. He had decided to leave full-time employment in order to become a contractor.

She recalls, *"Graham used an agency to secure the contracting role. Later he found out there were a couple of temp roles required at a client and after talking to a couple of contractors, he obtained their CVs. As a result of this, Capital Staffing was born! I bought a typewriter, some stationery for the company and over the weekend re-typed the CVs. On Monday our first placements were made!"*

At first, Silk juggled working full-time in her role at Phillips with the demands of placing contractors through Capital, but then she took

Karen is a country girl at heart, has a lifelong love for horses and enjoys showjumping and dressage.

the plunge and knew she had found the perfect vehicle to allow that family entrepreneurial spirit to flourish.

"I absolutely love recruitment where each day brings different challenges and given it is absolutely predicated on developing personal relationships, it is vital - for long term success - to put your values, including your integrity, compassion and honour at the centre of your business." Capital enjoyed sustained growth as it followed its clients' needs across the UK and mainland Europe. Husband Graham later joined the business full-time (in 1997) and at its height, Capital had a turnover in excess of £15 million and 45 staff. Creating an environment that fostered technical expertise and which allowed staff to develop a balance between work and personal life was and remains a critical element to Capital's success.

Silk comments, *"We took the conscious decision to be specialists rather than generalists and I remain passionate about our niche markets in defence, aerospace, automotive and telecommunications. We have also ensured our staff find Capital to be a fun and supportive place to work and I am proud that we have many that have been with us for many years. Two of my senior consultants, for example, have been with us 18 and 12 years respectively. This gives confidence to clients and also engenders deep expertise within our business."*

It is a point supported by academic research. In his 2002 book, *Leading Teams: Setting the Stage for Great Performances*, Harvard psychology professor, Richard Hackman, highlights that business team performance tends to be enhanced as shared tenure increases. Furthermore, stable teams develop what psychologist, Dan Wegner, calls 'transactive memory', which is that over time, team members understand the knowledge embedded amongst the team and recognise core strengths and weaknesses.

Silk's journey has, however, not been without its vicissitudes, both personal and business related.

Clearly, the 2008 global financial crisis was one that profoundly impacted Capital:

"We had survived several recessions prior to 2008 but I think virtually all across recruitment this was by far the most pervasive. Yes, it hit our numbers but we survived and fell back on the strength of our expertise and longevity of our client relationships. The last 30 years have taught us that recruitment is a two-way street and we have to find roles that ignite the passion of our candidates and match them with organisations competing for the very best talent to realise their corporate goals. You have to serve both constituencies with integrity and in today's transparent world, values matter."

As stated earlier, 2014 was a great year for Silk. Her memorable address at the Gender Diversity conference and election to the APSCo committee were external recognition of the contribution she has made to the world of recruitment and the business sectors Capital serves.

Unfortunately, in 2015 Silk faced profound personal tragedy. Shockingly both her mother and sister (the latter completely unexpectedly) passed away within seven days of each other.

"It has taken a year to recover from this and inevitably the business did suffer as I questioned whether I could come back from this deeply painful episode."

She is now back at the helm of the business and her verve and spirit was evident when we met at the Institute of Directors in April 2016. Happily, the business is now thriving and growing and Silk confirms, "I am confident about the future. Our brand and team is excellent and I feel privileged to help the UK and Europe meet its need for technical staff across strategically vital industry sectors."

Outside the world of business, Silk retains her lifelong love for horses and country pursuits and enjoys showjumping and dressage. She and husband Graham are proud parents of their 20-year-old daughter and 17-year-old son.

"WE TOOK THE CONSCIOUS DECISION TO BE SPECIALISTS RATHER THAN GENERALISTS AND I REMAIN PASSIONATE ABOUT OUR NICHE MARKETS.

JASON STEWART
CEO - DRC LOCUMS

J ason Stewart is the CEO of DRC Locums, one of the leading staffing agencies supplying doctors and nursing professionals to the NHS. The company has service level agreements with more than 100 individual trusts and offers both temporary and permanent recruitment solutions across all clinical specialisms. Headquartered in Milton Keynes the business employs more than 60 consultants.

I have been fortunate enough to meet Stewart several times recently and his insight and breadth of vision across the healthcare recruitment sector is clear. As he says, *"Healthcare recruitment is now facing many of the structural challenges encountered by other segments of the recruitment market over the past decade or*

I HAD A DRIVE TO WORK FROM CHILDHOOD AND WAS ALWAYS KEEN TO TAKE WEEKEND JOBS AT SCHOOL. I KNEW I WANTED TO BE INVOLVED IN BUSINESS."

so; the introduction of neutral vendors, structured buying environments and consolidation and margin pressure. This is what IT recruitment faced in the late 1990s and early 2000s. In addition, The DoH's agency rate cap is hitting the sector too of course!"

Over more than 16 years in recruitment Stewart has developed expertise in turnaround and change; these are perhaps the most challenging disciplines within any business as evidenced by the title of the book by business school scholars, Chip and Dan Heath, from 2011, entitled *Switch: How to Change Things when Change is Hard.*

A point of interest, however, is that Stewart spent nearly a decade in his 'first' career as a chartered accountant, although this wasn't a planned career path. He says, *"I was born in Vancouver and whilst my family was full of doctors I always had an entrepreneurial streak. I had a drive to work from childhood and was always keen to take weekend jobs at school. I knew I wanted to be involved in business."*

His father is British and Stewart moved back to the UK aged 13, eventually attending Newcastle University. He says, *"I studied Economics as it gave me a good grounding in broader business related issues. I then chose to qualify as a chartered accountant having been advised that finance is the language of business. Three years of exam hell while working full time was tough, I have to admit. Even more challenging was that I entered the jobs market in the teeth of the recession of the early 1990s."*

He has never forgotten that early dance with economic cycles: *"Competition for my first career move was very tough. It was a great lesson in ensuring that you should never be complacent in business."*

Stewart spent the 1990s as a chartered accountant and was involved in the sale of one of the UK's first internet start-ups, when in 1999 he was headhunted into MSB International. He tells me, *"I never had any intention of moving into recruitment! Interestingly as an IT-focused recruiter it was then facing the structural challenges which healthcare recruitment is experiencing now. This included margin erosion and my role was to develop new sectors for the business. It was a fast paced environment and my commercial bias toward sales aligned to my financial rigour helped me to thrive in the business."*

Acting as de facto sales director, Stewart managed 30 sales and resource people and three operations directors in the non-IT division of the business, which focused on finance and engineering market segments. He feels that whilst being very sales-orientated his accountancy training has been critical to his success as a recruitment leader.

As he explains, *"In my career I've seen so many of my contemporaries within recruitment struggle with an understanding of cash flows, P&Ls and the basic financial dynamics of their business. Without this understanding your job of running a recruitment business is so much harder. My training as a chartered accountant is invaluable to me every day in my role as CEO."*

His financial savvy was certainly a benefit as in 2006 he became involved with external partners in a bid for MSB as senior shareholders sought an exit from the business. *"Unfortunately Networkers International trumped our bid by a considerable margin,"* he explains. *"My backers were also shareholders so took the premium being offered. The whole process was an invaluable learning curve for me."*

Stewart's next move was in 2007 when he joined Redwood Group, a leading recruiter to the healthcare and technical sectors. As managing director his commercial experience was enhanced as he engaged in a buy and build growth strategy and managed a team of eight executives and 73 sales people. The business grew from £22 million turnover when he joined, to £55 million when he left in 2012.

He recalls, *"I led the sale of the respective healthcare and technical divisions to larger industry specialists. What was important was that I had exposure to the opportunities and challenges being afforded by the healthcare sector and knew that strategically this would be the market I wanted to focus on in my career."*

In 2012 Stewart's intimate knowledge of the market lead him to identify DRC Locums as an ideal opportunity where he could add value. *"DRC had experienced significant management change and a level of instability which had affected the performance of the business,"* he says.

07

He made an approach to Hamilton Bradshaw Private Equity and investors James Caan and Tristan Ramus clearly recognised they had the right leader to grow the business. Stewart adds, *"I know what I am good at and I identified that the main challenge was to stabilise the business and professionalise processes and platforms to build value. This struck the right chord with the investors and I was offered the role that day and began at DRC within a week"*

Much academic ink has been spilt in business schools seeking to set out the key steps to successfully executing change in a business. The Heath brothers in the book mentioned above (and in their earlier title *Made to Stick* (2007)) emphasise the importance of having a clear and rational plan for change but highlight that this is not enough; emotional buy-in to motivate a team is indispensable.

Jason concurs wholeheartedly, saying, *"I've seen too many turnarounds in recruitment where a business ends up being run like an insurance company losing all the entrepreneurial drive that provided its initial success. The key is absolutely ensuring that the proper controls and processes are in place whilst at the same time retaining the passion and drive of the sales team."*

Over the nearly four years since Stewart took over the helm at DRC it has grown and diversified. Already renowned for its locum expertise it took the strategic decision to enter the nursing market in 2013 and that part of the business underwent exponential growth.

As a whole the business has more than £40 million turnover and gross margin is rapidly rising. Stewart is always looking to grow new markets *("every CEO in recruitment should be sales savvy")* and the business is enhancing its penetration within the private healthcare sector.

Jason and his wife Elizabeth live in London and are proud parents to their daughter and when work permits, he and the family enjoy travel. He remains characteristically ebullient about the future: *"It is undeniable that healthcare recruitment is facing a period of extraordinary challenge and particularly in the next few months. But we have some of the best healthcare recruiters in the industry at DRC and are a framework supplier to the NHS. The unique and highly regulated environment in health provides unparalleled opportunities for those who get the business model right."*

"THE KEY IS ABSOLUTELY ENSURING THAT THE PROPER CONTROLS AND PROCESSES ARE IN PLACE WHILST AT THE SAME TIME RETAINING THE PASSION AND DRIVE OF THE SALES TEAM

STEVE INGHAM
CEO - PAGEGROUP

Steve Ingham is CEO of PageGroup (which operates three key brands: Page Executive, Michael Page and Page Personnel).

Steve Ingham is an impressive chap; exuding gravitas and commanding one's complete attention from the moment one meets him. Something to be expected of the CEO of a business with more than 5500 employees, £513 million in gross profit (2013) and 155 global offices, I guess. But the numbers are only part of the story; there is also the focus and passion of the man. *"I am proud to be CEO of PageGroup, which I consider to be the world's most impressive professional recruitment company,"* Steve says with relish.

I SOON DECIDED THAT BEING SEALED AWAY IN A SCIENCE LAB WAS NOT CONSISTENT WITH MY PERSONAL ATTRIBUTES AND SO JOINED THE SALES AND MARKETING DEPARTMENT."

Interestingly, Steve's working life began in the world of science, far from the commercial vibrancy of recruitment.

"I completed my degree in metallurgy and material science at Nottingham University and joined Johnson Matthey as a graduate trainee. I soon decided that being sealed away in a science lab was not consistent with my personal attributes and so joined the sales and marketing department," Steve explains.

He remained with the materials giant for four years and then through friends learned of an opportunity at PageGroup (formerly known as Michael Page International): *"I realised that there was an entrepreneurial spark within me seeking a truly meritocratic environment in which to flourish. I secured an interview with Michael Page at a time when it was diversifying from its core finance market. I joined Michael Page Marketing and Sales as a consultant in 1987."*

The rest, as they say, is history. Within three years Steve was an operating director and was appointed managing director within marketing and sales by 1994. He then took additional responsibilities across the business and joined the board as executive director of UK in 2001. In April 2006, he was appointed CEO.

As he approaches his ninth year as CEO I ask him to reflect on some of the key themes of his journey to the top of a world class brand: *"I am particularly proud that as we tackled the twin challenges of scale and international expansion we have maintained a long term vision and adherence to core values,"* Steve explains. *"Whilst I was, and remain, very proud to be CEO of such a great business I am also particularly proud that I, like most of our senior leadership team, began here as a consultant."*

I asked Steve to elaborate on the way in which PageGroup has been able to develop such longevity amongst its top performers, particularly in a sector perceived to have high turnover. *"We ensure we have the best and most experienced home grown talent in each key role, and our team-based structure and primarily profit share business model is a cornerstone of this. As we expand organically and invest in a new area, we do so only with a long-term objective and in the knowledge that at some point there will be periods of economic slowdown."*

This approach clearly enabled PageGroup to traverse the 2008 recession as it had a very strong balance sheet (£138 million in cash) at the time. Indeed, between 2009 and 2013 it saw its revenues climb from lows of £716 million to over £1 billion.

Its profit before tax hiked from £21 million to £64 million (excluding exceptional items). The company's long term vision has permitted it to expand in key international markets as it diversifies its footprint by geography and discipline. Steve sees significant opportunity in Greater China, South East Asia, Germany, Latin America and the USA.

Steve studied science at Nottingham University and has a degree in metallurgy and material science.

I also ask Steve to comment on the nature of recruitment today and the view that some digital platforms may severely encroach on the sector:

"When I began there were pages and pages of roles in print media. Today, recruitment via print media is virtually extinct as use of digital and social media platforms has become universal, but it remains a channel, not a true alternative. In a world where the competition amongst employers for high quality talent is fiercer than ever, the need for expert professional recruitment partners is critical. Our culture of developing teams with deep expertise within a vertical ensures we are a partner of choice for employers nationally and internationally."

Outside of his responsibilities as CEO at PageGroup, Steve is a non-executive director at Debenhams plc and also a member of the Corporate Partnership board at Great Ormond Street Hospital.

"I REALISED THAT THERE WAS AN ENTREPRENEURIAL SPARK WITHIN ME SEEKING A TRULY MERITOCRATIC ENVIRONMENT IN WHICH TO FLOURISH.

08

BLUE OCEANS
IMAGINATION

A thought experiment: if your business comes out top in industry benchmarking surveys, does this mean you have a winning strategy? Perhaps. Does it mean your 'lead' position or competitive advantage is assured to be sustainable: most definitely not.

As we have seen, successful strategy is about differentiation from competitors to capture more of the value in the market and this is where the notion of finding a 'blue ocean' comes in. In their multi-million bestselling book from 2005, *Blue Ocean Strategy* by W. Chan Kim and Renée Mauborgne, both professors at INSEAD, one of the world's leading business schools, argue that most companies fight in the 'red ocean' where there is little real differentiation and margins continually erode.

This of course describes many segments of the recruitment sector where we have seen a substantial rise of new entrants into a particular market which has been delivering high margins (financial services and healthcare recruitment come to mind) which in turn leads to more fighting for the slice of the pie and over time, reductions in margins.

Kim and Mauborgne suggest that creative thinking can lead to discovery of relatively uncontested markets - 'blue oceans' where by definition the uniqueness of the service offering generates high profitability. It seems a simple idea but in reality it is fiendishly difficult to execute and some business scholars have cast doubt on the very idea of securing even a relatively temporary competitive advantage in today's globalised and data-rich competitive world.

Others have argued you may not need to find a whole new 'blue ocean' but instead expand your business at the 'edges' of the markets in which it operates. This is the thesis of a new book (*Edge Strategy: A new mindset for profitable growth* 2016) which includes the suggestion of investing in deep understanding of the 'customer journey'. This in turn can lead to an expansion of your range of services to address each step of the journey. One can see this philosophy underpinning the growth of RPO offerings which seek to address the whole resourcing needs of a client as opposed to periodic contingent talent requirements.

The leaders in this chapter have embraced the idea of creating distinctive service offerings whether of the 'blue ocean' or 'edge' variety.

Gary Ashworth for example in 2001 when establishing InterQuest (the second start-up recruitment business he has listed on the stock exchange; his first being Abacus which he set up aged 21!) in the technology markets was adamant always to look ahead to identify niche markets. *"I always ask what happens after what happens next,"* and this obsession with imaginatively interpreting the markets he operates within has kept Gary at the very summit of successful recruiters for decades.

Creating a 'blue ocean' strategy does not necessarily involve re-inventing the wheel, however, and includes having the imagination to think about current offerings and models and through even small incremental adjustments deliver the much sought after *"unique mix of value"* Professor Michael Porter describes.

This was precisely the creative genius Adam Buck called upon when, after a successful career at SThree, he set up Selby Jennings (the first brand in what is now the multi-sector and award winning international recruiter Phaidon International). Its aim was specifically to offer a 'disruptive' model involving combining the flexibility of contingent recruitment with the structured approach of Search in the financial market space. Phaidon has continued to identify micro niche segments in complementary markets to differentiate itself.

Professors Kim and Mauborgne offer a deceptively simple (albeit powerful) set of questions to consider when searching for the promised land of a 'blue ocean' which they call their Four Actions Framework. This invites business leaders to step back and challenge the accepted wisdom of their particular markets and as the Professors say *"...industry structure is not given: it can be shaped."* The questions include asking which accepted practices in an industry can be eliminated, which can be reduced, which can be raised into more prominence and finally what can be created that is new for the industry?

Andrea Williams, soon after taking up the role as MD at Ambition's UK business in 2012, decided that she wanted to exit some contracts within the banking sector that had become antithetical to her strategy even if such contracts generated volume and high profile client names.

Personifying perhaps more the 'edge strategy' David Rai is a leader who likes to ensure the odds in business are in his favour. He co-founded Testing Circle to operate in the highly specialised field of testing software markets and has now expanded the business to include not only recruitment services but broader consultancy services to clients.

Joost Kreulen (whose journey within recruitment began more than 30 years ago after a chance meeting in his native Netherlands when he was unable to pursue his original career in hotel management in the US), the CEO at global recruiter Empresaria Group has taken the advice to seek out uncontested markets quite literally. The archetypal intrepid traveller, under his leadership Empresaria has opened in many countries around the world where recruitment as a sector is at a nascent stage.

Celebrated Harvard Business School Professor Youngme Moon, in her 2011 book *Different: Escaping the Competitive Herd* exhorts business leaders to remember how critical developing a unique value proposition is for their businesses:

"...in category after category, companies have gotten so collectively locked into a particular cadence of competition that they appear to have lost sight of their mandate- which is to create meaningful grooves of separation from one another."

And it is accurate to say that Andy Larholt founded Montash with such a mandate to offer differentiated expertise, originally as a SAP specialist when it began in 2004, then within the crowded and fiercely competitive world of IT recruitment.

GARY ASHWORTH
CHAIRMAN
INTERQUEST
GROUP PLC

To found and launch one stock exchange listed recruitment business is impressive; to do so twice is plain showing off! Gary Ashworth, a bona fide legend within recruitment, has achieved this and is currently chairman at InterQuest, the listed IT and related markets specialist, which in 2014 delivered a turnover of £150 million and a 33% rise in NFI (Net Foreign Investment) to £23.2 million.

I met Ashworth at The Club at The Ivy and asked what drives him, to which he replied, *"Insecurity! More accurately, the drive to create security throughout my life. I was given up for adoption at just six weeks old and that has always been a driver of ambition."*

A COLLEAGUE AND I DECIDED WE COULD DO THIS OURSELVES AND AGED 21 I SET UP ABACUS IN A SHABBY OFFICE ABOVE A PUB IN THE CITY. THE EC4 POSTCODE WAS IMPORTANT."

Ashworth was brought up in Marlow, Buckinghamshire and values a close family for obvious reasons. *"My nest is important to me. I was blessed with a lovely upbringing by my adoptive parents and my sister and I are still very close."* His entrepreneurial flame was lit early. At 12, being creative about his age, he secured a paper round earning £1.40 per week, while at 15 he began a lifelong interest in the creative arts when he promoted a pop concert.

Shortly thereafter he entered recruitment. *"'The Evening Standard' was full of adverts from recruitment businesses offering alluring commissions and I couldn't believe you could earn a fortune from chatting to people so I applied for some jobs."* For three years Ashworth excelled, moving through the ranks within a business in the finance and banking sectors, then he made a bold move.

As he explains, *"A colleague and I decided we could do this ourselves and aged 21 I set up Abacus in a shabby office above a pub in the City. The EC4 postcode was important."* However, he adds, *"I do not think it was courageous given I had no responsibilities, mortgage or children, just bags full of passion."*

The business thrived and after two years he bought out his partner. Sheer hard work and the ability to spot talent in people led to Ashworth growing Abacus and the business eventually floated on AIM in 1995 (the year the junior market was created). He sold the business for £17 million to Lord Ashcroft's Carlisle Holdings in 1999.

He elaborates, *"I was 39 and had two young children at the time but was divorced so decided to go travelling to Miami for six months where I set up a property company and had lots of fun. It was like Disneyland for grown ups!"* He had by this time met Luke Johnson, the celebrated entrepreneur, who remains a key business partner and who took a stake in InterQuest when it was launched in 2001. Ashworth says, *"I believe strongly in researching markets and trends to identify what happens 'after what happens next'. It was clear that technology, and micro niches within it, were sectors with exponential potential and so InterQuest was born."*

The business thrived, floating on AIM in 2005. It currently employs over 300 people and has an enterprise value approaching £50 million. Ashworth reflects, *"One of the key lessons I have learned particularly with InterQuest and its markets is you have to continually innovate to differentiate yourself and outpace your competition. Currently this includes creating unique content to access a unique talent pool of candidates who can be brokered at 'above industry' margins. Paradoxically you have to accept that today's niche may become tomorrow's commodity offering."*

Through more than 30 years of entrepreneurship, Ashworth has retained a profound interest in the creative world of arts, producing plays and managing jazz singers and comedians. He says, *"There may be little money in it but I believe that business people have a duty to give back to the arts since they tend to spark ideas and have naïve enthusiasm that can often cross over into commerce."*

His artistic pursuits include financially supporting the Assembly Rooms at the Edinburgh Festival and he is rightly proud of producing

the play 'Anonymous Society' which won best overall production at
the Edinburgh Festival Fringe in 1999.

Despite creating two successful listed recruitment businesses
Ashworth's passion for the sector and his keen eye for spotting the
potential in people led him to set up Recruitment Capital Partners
in the summer of 2014. *"The raison d'etre of Recruitment Capital
Partners (RCP) is to support recruitment professionals with the
passion to build scalable businesses and who want to be treated
fairly in the process. Being ethical as an investor is critical and chimes
with the values I believe should govern the recruitment sector."*

He affirms, *"I remain driven as my passion for business is
undiminished and I have an unnatural fear that it all might somehow
be taken away one day. I am, however, now proud to help the next
generation of entrepreneurs through RCP and also continue to
indulge my interest in creative endeavours through writing projects
and supporting artists."* I for one would not exclude the possibility of
this legendary recruiter creating a third listed business in the next
few years... watch this space.

"I BELIEVE STRONGLY IN RESEARCHING MARKETS AND TRENDS TO IDENTIFY WHAT HAPPENS 'AFTER WHAT HAPPENS NEXT'.

08

ADAM BUCK
CEO - PHAIDON INTERNATIONAL

Adam Buck is the founder and CEO of award winning global recruitment business, Phaidon International. The company encompasses eight micro-specialist brands across its four core vertical markets which comprise financial services, energy, professional services and STEM (incorporating life sciences and telecommunications). Employing more than 300 people and with offices in Europe and North America, as well the Asia Pacific Region, the business places talent across more than 60 countries and in 2014 delivered £21.8 million in NFI (Net Foreign Investment) and an EBITDA of £3.6 million.

IT HAS BEEN AN AMAZING JOURNEY, NOT WITHOUT CHALLENGES OF COURSE, BUT I DO PINCH MYSELF GIVEN I BEGAN THE SELBY JENNINGS BUSINESS WORKING FROM MY BEDROOM IN 2004!"

I catch up with Buck at the company's headquarters based in the heart of London. He is excited about the continued growth of the business which he began with the Selby Jennings brand in 2004. Phaidon won numerous awards in 2014 including Best Small Company to Work For, *The Sunday Times* and International Recruitment Company of the Year *Recruitment International*. Buck tells me, *"It has been an amazing journey, not without challenges of course, but I do pinch myself given I began the Selby Jennings business working from my bedroom in 2004!"*

One of the most influential business books of the past decade is *Blue Ocean Strategy* written by W. Chan Kim and Renée Mauborgne. In it they argue that most companies compete in a 'red ocean'; in an overcrowded market, where margins are continually driven down. Kim and Mauborgne suggest that to succeed the key is to differentiate one's offering to establish presence in an uncontested market (the 'Blue Ocean') where margins are greater.

It appears Buck and Phaidon have been aiming to so differentiate; as Buck explains, *"Recruitment is a highly commoditised industry. On the surface there is little scope for differentiation but through a number of small and inter-related advantages, which together amount to one significant competitive advantage, Phaidon has excelled."* Phaidon prides itself on having true insight and offering clients 'micro-specialist' expertise across its brands. In addition, as the brands are closely related, it offers clients one stop solutions to their talent needs.

Buck's entrepreneurial energy seems to be in his DNA. As he says, *"My father is a self-made businessperson who left school at 14 and eventually set up his own printing business. I was fortunate to be the first in my family to go to a private school. This offered me an academic advantage but also exposure to a world of success and privilege that made me hungry to be successful myself. In fact, from an early age I was always attracted by doing deals and the world of business. This included buying discounted branded clothing and reselling it to my teachers at school! I guess I always knew that one day I would run my own business".*

He graduated with a politics degree from Loughborough University and then entered the world of work with a Kent-based firm in the office furniture sector. It was to be a short lived career. *"I quickly worked out that even with significant sales growth the business would struggle to offer the type of rewards that I wanted. So I went to see the managing director to test my hypothesis and asked him how much he earned; his answer lead me to immediately leave the business and seek reward elsewhere!"*

His sales flair and charisma lead to several offers from recruitment firms and, after being interviewed by Gary Elden for a role at Huxley (part of SThree), he joined the banking and finance, engineering and energy and ICT specialist in 1998. *"It was the ideal environment,"* says Buck, *"In my first full year I was the top biller at Huxley within its permanent division.*

This was IT recruitment but I had very quickly noticed that the telecoms sector was experiencing great growth and established Orgtel as one of the new SThree brands to build out this offering for the group."

The early 2000s were, however, also a period of challenge with the bursting of the tech bubble and, in the period following the sale of 3G telecom licences, significant reductions in hiring by the leading telecom providers such as Motorola. Indeed, Buck says, *"It was a learning curve. It showed me how, without diversification, a solid business could easily face challenges if over-dependent on too few markets or clients."*

By this time, he had begun to diversify with Orgtel, offering specialist talent within the financial services/banking space. In 2004 he took a step back and decided that it was the right time to set up his own business and his philosophy was one that Professors Kim and Mauborgne would approve of in terms of 'Blue Ocean' thinking. He recalls, *"Leaving SThree was tough in one sense as it was a great business where I learned so much. But having specialised in permanent recruitment I could see that clients in the banking world would hugely benefit from the flexibility of a contingent recruitment model but with the structured approach of retained search. It was a disruptive approach but I knew that by keeping up front costs to a minimum and yet still delivering the highly niche talent being sought this model would differentiate us."*

In 2004 Buck started Selby Jennings (his grandmothers' respective maiden names) from his bedroom and with a fax, PC and telephone (and no database!) he generated £700,000 NFI on his own. That he

sometimes worked the phones from his 'office' wearing only pyjamas on some days is the stuff they don't teach you at business school!

"We grew hugely over the 2004-2008 period when we hit £5 million NFI and by that time Selby Jennings had 35 people. All our business was UK focused. The credit crunch then offered another rapid business lesson! Lehman disappeared and our candidate interview volume fell 80% in a heartbeat."

It was at this point he made the decision to 'follow the candidates' and diversify both geographically and in terms of market coverage. He says, *"The underlying approach was to offer the same disruptive model of contingent flexibility with a structured search methodology to under-brokered and overpriced niche markets and to do so globally."*

DSJ Global was established as the first professional services brand in 2008. In 2011 Carlton Senior Appointments (serving the wealth management sector) and Viridium Associates (renewable energy) were created. *"In 2012 we opened our office in Singapore and added the New York and Zurich offices the following year. Hong Kong became our second APAC office in 2014 and San Francisco our second US office in 2015. More than 85% of our business is now outside the UK,"* Buck tells me.

Buck expects Phaidon's astounding growth (it has grown more than 30% year on year) to continue and believes that, as well as its differentiated micro specialist based offering, the values of the business permit a growing workforce to cohere into a true team. He says, *"I started my career journey in recruitment to create a successful career for myself, this ambition soon grew into the ambition to create exceptional careers for others and I find developing and investing the talent that joins Phaidon really rewarding."*

He cites loyalty as being fundamental to Phaidon's success, saying, *"At the centre of our organic culture is loyalty. We offer an environment through our award winning training programme that allows smart and motivated people to flourish. 90% of senior management began as graduates with us."*

Outside work Buck is a busy family man, he and his wife (whom he met while at Huxley) live in South West London with their four children (all aged under 10). He retains an avid interest in politics and sport, but spends most of his free time as a taxi driver for his children. *"I still love what I do and helping the next generation of leaders take the business forward is a hugely rewarding way to spend my business life."* One suspects many more awards and stories of expansion await Buck and Phaidon.

"I STILL LOVE WHAT I DO AND HELPING THE NEXT GENERATION OF LEADERS TAKE THE BUSINESS FORWARD IS A HUGELY REWARDING WAY TO SPEND MY BUSINESS LIFE.

ANDREA WILLIAMS
MANAGING DIRECTOR
AMBITION

Since 2012 Andrea has been UK managing director of Ambition, a leading global boutique recruitment business headquartered in Australia. She has held leadership positions within recruitment in Australia and the Far East. However, she explains her first profession was actually teaching.

"Following my sports science degree I became a PE teacher and rose to head of PE within four years. I had always had a desire to live in Australia and I took the plunge and emigrated in 1994." Andrea stumbled across an advert for a recruitment role whilst still having every intention of securing a teaching position.

HEALTHY COMPETITION WAS A NATURAL VALUE FOR ME AND I BECAME A TOP BILLER AND WAS RECOGNISED BY BEING PROMOTED TO MANAGEMENT."

The call she made changed her professional destiny. *"I called Nick Waterworth (who later co-founded Ambition) who was then the MD for Michael Page in Australia. After nine, yes nine, interviews I got the role."* She began as a consultant dealing with temporary assignments within the banking and finance sectors. She stayed with Michael Page for more than four years and then had a further three years within banking and finance recruitment. She excelled and the discipline, focus and competitiveness of her grounding in sports were an aid to her swift climb into management. She says, *"I loved the buzz of recruitment and the meritocracy appealed to my sense of fairness. Healthy competition was a natural value for me and I became a top biller and was recognised by being promoted to management."*

By this time Ambition had been founded in 1999 by Nick Waterworth and Paul Lyons, and recalling Andrea's success at Michael Page nearly a decade earlier she was invited to become director of banking and finance. Andrea elaborates, *"I was responsible for both permanent and temporary recruitment. Two years later I was given responsibility for the Hong Kong office, led the creation of the Singapore office in 2007 and then in 2008 became MD of the Hong Kong office."*

Andrea enjoyed seven successful years with Ambition focusing on securing growth and the challenge of steering the business through the global financial crisis. In 2010 Andrea left the company having decided to relocate back to the UK. But her destiny seems to be tied to Ambition and in the summer of 2012 she was appointed as managing director of the UK business based in London.

The London business serves two main client verticals; professional services clients (across finance and accounting, business development and marketing and business support) and also financial services (across finance and accounting and operations) and her role was not only to grow the operation but also deal with integration of the Witan Jardine business which Ambition had acquired and re-branded prior to Andrea's appointment as managing director. She explains:

"There were important post-integration legacy issues to resolve following the acquisition. In addition, given the huge challenges for all recruiters in the financial services space, there was a need to take some tough and long term decisions. Ambition's purpose is to build better futures and base this on integrity. One of the key decisions I made was to exit some large banking client agreements that did not align with our vision."

Two years after taking the helm the London business is thriving, has a turnover in excess of £10 million and employs 50 people. Within the financial services sectors Ambition has been developing innovative service delivery models leveraging a symbiotic relationship between business development and talent acquisition consultation.

Andrea points out that another market Ambition serves is the legal profession which is itself facing a period of significant change. *"Legal*

Andrea had NINE interviews before she was accepted by Michael Page in Australia.

businesses are facing unprecedented change including the nature of the client relationship. This includes the importance of intelligent use of data and leveraging of digital platforms to enhance brand. We are partnering with firms to find this talent for these critical areas." Andrea is confident that Ambition's values, vision and versatility of its people bode well for the future.

She is undoubtedly an impressive professional in the competitive world of recruitment and confirms she has not entirely lost the link to her PE past, saying, *"I retain my passion for sport and run several miles to and from work a few times each week. I am also looking to develop my interest in cycling at weekends."* Drive and passion are two foundational values for Ambition and Andrea, whether in sport or business, clearly walks (or should I say runs) her talk!

"AMBITION'S PURPOSE IS TO BUILD BETTER FUTURES AND BASE THIS ON INTEGRITY.

DAVID RAI
CEO - TESTING CIRCLE

David, co-founder and CEO of Testing Circle, the IT recruiter specialising in software testing solutions, did not start commercial life as a recruiter. I met him in Mayfair not far from his old stomping ground in the world of gambling and high rollers.

"After I completed my MSc in Management at Manchester University I landed a role with Rank Organisation in London in 1997. It was bright lights and big city and I had huge fun and learned a lot about sales and life!" David reminisces.

His suave manner, Hollywood smile and effortless charm make it easy to believe he excelled in that world. *"I was able to generate more than £6 million of revenue for the London*

IT IS HARD TO OVER-ESTIMATE THE IMPORTANCE OF THIS MARKET AND INDEED ITS POTENTIAL SIZE AS TECHNOLOGY SYSTEMS BECOME MORE COMPLEX."

Casino Estate and remained in that business for three years," David adds.

His entrepreneurial and sales flair took him all over the world for the next few years. He co-founded Online Gambling Organisation, a multi-platform gaming solution. He relocated to Beverly Hills (living the dream!) and helped raise more than £1 million in private funding for the business.

"It was a great few years and the opportunity to work internationally was exciting and rewarding. Unfortunately, due to US legislation relating to preventing online gambling solutions I sold out my interests and took on other challenges." His knowledge of the importance of getting IT/online infrastructure right within the gaming sector alerted him to the potential of supplying testing talent within the broader software development market.

"Testing has been called 'IT's Invisible Giant' and whilst many commentators have called this the next big thing it - the need to ensure software is optimally functional - has been around for ages," David explains. It is hard to over-estimate the importance of this market and indeed its potential size as technology systems become more complex, the demand for ever swifter and more accurate functionality rises and new applications (web based, mobile and others) for business are created.

08

"It has been estimated that the software testing market is worth more than $50 billion. Given maybe a third of projects are actually successful and the need to ensure testing budgets are spent on minimising project failures, I am confident that the market will continue to grow."

David has brought his commercial and sales acumen from his international business experience within gaming to Testing Circle and helped it to grow. Indeed, Testing Circle grew its revenue from £300,000 to £4 million in its first two years of business. *"Then came the recession and it was a challenging period for the whole recruitment sector and despite the central mission-critical importance of testing our growth spurt naturally took a hit."* But given the fundamentals of the testing market in recent years Testing Circle has grown considerably and now delivers a turnover in excess of £7 million and has ambitious plans of further growth in the next 24 months.

David took the strategic decision to strengthen the Board to help with these growth plans and this year announced that Jonathan Wright had been appointed advisor to the Board. Jonathan is of course very well known as an international recruiter having been Group CEO for Alexander Mann for 10 years. David is delighted with the appointment: *"We see the appointment of Jonathan as integral to realising our ambitious growth plans."* Jonathan is clearly excited about Testing Circle: *"Testing Circle is a prominent example of current thinking in Human Capital Strategy; specialist, knowledge-driven and focused on customer outcomes."* Testing Circle, it should be noted, offers a range of services to clients.

David Rai began working life amidst the glitz of the world of gambling with high rollers and even set up his own online gaming business.

Its recruitment practice offers talent acquisition services to a number of sectors including financial services, media, mobile and retail. In addition, its consultancy arm offers cost effective Software and Systems Testing managed services to enterprise and mid-market businesses.

David's journey in business has taken him all around the world from the world of high rolling gamblers in London to leading a niche recruitment and consultancy business within a multi-billion testing market set to grow further. Outside of business David and his wife are expecting the arrival of their first child and perhaps that might mellow this charismatic international businessman; but somehow I suspect it will spur him on ever more toward reaching the ambitious plans for Testing Circle. ⌐

"TESTING CIRCLE IS A PROMINENT EXAMPLE OF CURRENT THINKING IN HUMAN CAPITAL STRATEGY; SPECIALIST, KNOWLEDGE-DRIVEN AND FOCUSED ON CUSTOMER OUTCOMES.

ANDREW LARHOLT
CEO - MONTASH

In March 2014 Andy travelled to the US to receive the prestigious 'Best Staffing Firm to Work For' award from the Staffing Industry Analysts. It is less than a decade since he founded Montash, the specialist IT recruiter, working from a single man office with no windows!

Whilst that has been quite a journey - see more below - Andy's recruitment career began even earlier in 1998; astonishing given his youthful looks!

"I fell into recruitment at the age of 19 and joined Huxley's City of London team. I was hooked. The energy of the place and the meritocracy suited my work ethic and ambition ideally." Andy recalls.

THE COMPANY HAD BECOME MUCH MORE CORPORATE AND WITH OUTSIDE INVESTORS TO REPORT TO I FELT MY ENTREPRENEURIAL FLAIR WAS BEING CONSTRAINED."

In a meteoric six year rise he became European Recruitment Contracts Director focusing on the interim/temp contract market. He established and grew the team from scratch and oversaw the opening of offices in Germany and the Netherlands.

Interestingly he decided to leave at that point and had the courage to set up on his own.

"The company had become much more corporate and with outside investors to report to I felt my entrepreneurial flair was being constrained. Hindsight tells me I should have waited until the market float- it would have been financially lucrative for me - but I followed my instinct and decided to set up on my own"

So Montash began in 2004 and has experienced double digit growth every year since. Its offices are located in trendy Shoreditch and in 2013 the business's turnover exceeded £23 million and expects to top £30 million this year. It has assignments in 30 countries.

Andy is adamant that the combination of enduring values and excellent core expertise explain Montash's success - even through the recession - and its respect in the competitive IT staffing sector: *"What is the differentiator in a market - IT recruitment - where much of the supply is commoditised? I took the decision from the creation of the business that it had to be based around developing consultants who were real experts in their niche markets - whether ERP or Information Security - and not generalists posing as such. Wedded to this was a set of core values that all at Montash truly adhere to including 'excellence in everything we do.'"*

Part of Andy's commitment to ensuring the highest professionalism for Montash is to take Corporate Governance very seriously and this is reflected in the extensive experience and calibre of his Board. This includes non-executive advisors Leon Schumacher and Alex Arnot. Leon has a breadth of international C-suite experience in businesses such as Arcelor Mittal and Novartis. Alex is well known within recruitment with 20 years of success, including being a co-founder of Elite Leaders.

Andy explains: *"When you set up a business from scratch having come from a large successful business like Huxley, it is sometimes easy to take for granted the years of trial and error that took place to create the systems, infrastructure and internal know-how and composition of managerial boards that helped support the growth/sales function of the business."*

Andy was therefore committed to have a management team of the highest calibre to support the philosophy of meritocracy within Montash:

"I am passionate about providing development opportunities to everyone at Montash whether recruitment consultant or 'back office'. The culture encourages setting and surpassing goals with the vision

Andy left a really successful career at SThree to risk it all and set up his own business.

that the breadth and depth of the management team is always seeking to improve the service offering of Montash."

This foundation ensures that clients gain the benefit of an agile, pro-active leadership team and consultants that deliver expert high quality service. It is no accident that Montash works with world class brands such as Unilever, BP and AstraZeneca.

I have had the privilege of meeting Andy several times in recent months and he personifies what the recruitment sector (indeed any sector of business) seeks in its ambassadors - as all CEOs are - namely passionate commitment to excellence, a razor-sharp intellect and the desire to improve the experience for all who deal with Montash, whether staff or clients. Andy has ambitious targets for the business in the next 24 months and who would doubt he and Montash reach them?

"IT IS NO ACCIDENT THAT MONTASH WORKS WITH WORLD CLASS BRANDS SUCH AS UNILEVER, BP AND ASTRAZENECA.

JOOST KREULEN
CEO - EMPRESARIA GROUP PLC

J oost Kreulen is CEO of Empresaria, a position he has held since 2012. Empresaria is a global recruitment business operating across 18 brands and 18 countries. It employs more than 900 people and has turnover in excess of £187 million. It focuses on a number of sectors including construction, engineering, banking and finance, as well as logistics and IT.

'Strategy' is a key subject across business schools worldwide and many of the principles of strategy are derived from centuries of experience from military history. One of the seminal figures of military strategy is Carl von Clausewitz, a 19th-century Prussian officer, who posited that a key attribute of

I GOT THE OFFICE KEYS AND WITH NO INDUCTION BEGAN MY RECRUITMENT CAREER."

leaders is the ability to use intuition and grab opportunities in fluid circumstances; he called it coup d'oeil ('stroke of the eye').

Kreulen's recruitment career seems replete with examples of seizing such opportunities including his entrance into the industry.

"I am Dutch and after graduating from Hotel Management School in Maastricht in 1984 I ventured to the USA and worked for the Sheraton Group in Birmingham, Alabama. Unfortunately, my application for a Green Card was declined," Kreulen recalls.

Finding himself back in the Netherlands and in a recession he met a friend for a drink one Saturday evening and said he was looking for a job.

"My friend mentioned the staffing sector and frankly I knew nothing about it. Within 36 hours I had been introduced to the owner of Staff Planning. He overlooked my complete lack of experience and hired me to manage one of his branches in the south of the country. I got the office keys and with no induction began my recruitment career. I even had to explain what the industry was to my father after I had taken the role!"

Kreulen's ability to connect with and understand clients and candidates led to rapid success and within three years he grew Staff Planning, becoming regional manager in the process. Venture capitalists acquired the business in 1990 and, working to a five-year plan, Kreulen built it into a national multi-brand recruiter across 10 branches and was appointed managing director.

"Those early years were exhilarating and some of the best of my business life. I got such profound satisfaction at being instrumental in helping people find new roles; this is such a pivotal part of life - it provides the economic foundation for their families - that we in recruitment must never forget its importance for candidates. I was also inspired helping businesses find the talent they needed."

Staff Planning was acquired by Select Appointments plc in 1997 as the latter sought to move into the Dutch specialist staffing market. Kreulen spent the next decade or so (seven years under Select and then four years with Vedior after its $1.8 billion acquisition of Select) developing a multi-brand strategy of expansion.

"I was managing director in Netherlands and then the Nordic Zone too with Select. The beauty of the multi-brand strategy was that each brand focused on a specific sector; this allowed each to truly develop a differentiator by becoming an in-depth expert in its market segment. This provided substantive value adds for clients and candidates."

Kreulen was exposed to new challenges with Vedior as managing director and this included moving into new markets internationally including leading the M&A team to execute a 'buy and build' strategy in Germany between 2006-07.

"This entire period was one that afforded not only great personal development in terms of skills and opportunities; but, given I was overseeing a team of 10 managing directors across 12 operating companies (turning over 200 million euro) at Vedior, I was also able to help enable and empower talented colleagues

to realise their potential. This has been one of the highs of my recruitment career."

It was however at this point that Kreulen had to face a period of a relative 'low' in his commercial life and then exercise his version of coup d'oeil to strike out on a new challenge.

In 2008 Vedior was taken over by Randstad. Whereas Vedior was focused on multi-branding, the latter's strategy favoured mono-branding and integration. This meant that after so many years of hard work in the Netherlands to create a profitable multi-brand business the edifice was dismantled.

"The business I had built fell apart and it was a personal low. Fortunately, I was contacted at this point by Tony Martin whom I had known for many years (he was executive chairman at Select and Vedior) and invited to join Empresaria."

Kreulen was immediately at home with Empresaria's multi-brand model and took up the role as head of Asian operations in 2009. He oversaw multiple group companies across eight different countries and helped develop and identify new investments in the Asian region including India, China, Japan, Philippines, Thailand, Singapore, Malaysia and Indonesia.

He was appointed CEO in 2012 and is proud of Empresaria's reputation as a truly global recruiter.

"Empresaria had taken the strategic decision to expand into the AsiaPacific market in 2005-07 and this was important and remains

important in our performance given the disproportionate impact of the 2008 financial crisis within developed (particularly Eurozone) markets. Pre-2008 our NFI was 90% derived from the UK and European markets. Today it is split equally approximately across these and the Asia-Pacific markets."

The ability to understand and flourish across different cultures is a mark of business leadership in a global economy where it can be easy to forget how distinctive and deeply embedded local culture remains, despite all the talk of 'commodification' of culture in the 21st century.

Indeed, one of the most cited researchers in the world, Kreulen's countryman, Geert Hofstede in his book *Cultures and Organisations* has developed ground breaking tools to measure culture and makes this very point. Kreulen has long understood this key lesson, telling me,

"Empresaria continues to expand as a truly global recruiter. In the first half of 2014 for example, we opened offices in Hong Kong and Mexico and invested in a specialist staffing business in Dubai. Understanding local culture is vital particularly in markets where the staffing market is at a nascent stage of evolution. In Indonesia for example we sought to hire graduates and held open days for them and their families to attend and understand what the staffing sector was given so few even knew of it! It reminded me of the conversation I had had with my father nearly three decades earlier!"

Outside recruitment Kreulen is fond of golf (but complains of having too little time) and is a proud father of two children. His son is a trained psychologist and his daughter graduated from university in 2014. He and his wife Wilma also have a love of Spain and travel there often.

Kreulen, who is fluent in Dutch, German and English, is a shining example of a global citizen and business leader and his enthusiasm for staffing remains undiminished.

"I have been privileged in my recruitment career. Working with great people and helping clients and candidates. Never in my wildest dreams all those years ago in 1984 when I stumbled into the sector did I believe I would travel the world and learn so much."

"The lessons learned have not only brought the highs - and odd low mentioned above - but enabled me, in conjunction with local hospitals in Amsterdam between 2006-9, to co-found 'Emma at Work'; this is a not for profit staffing firm in the Netherlands which specialises in helping young people aged 16-25 suffering chronic diseases to find part time temporary work."

I have no doubt Kreulen's talents would have meant he excelled as a hotelier and being declined a Green Card was a disappointment for him but the recruitment sector has clearly been the richer for it!

"I GOT SUCH PROFOUND SATISFACTION AT BEING INSTRUMENTAL IN HELPING PEOPLE FIND NEW ROLES.

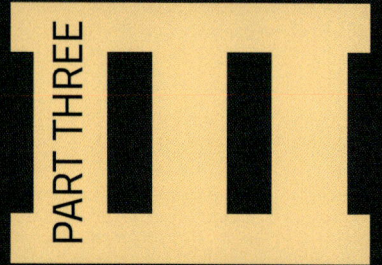

PART THREE

THE FUTURE IS HAPPENING NOW

CHAPTERS

09 **216-221**
LESSONS FROM **THE LEADERS**

10 **222-227**
THE FUTURE OF RECRUITMENT **IS HERE NOW**

228-231
FINAL THOUGHT: **THE MEDIUM IS THE MESSAGE**

232-233
BIBLIOGRAPHY **AND REFERENCES**

234-235
COMMENTS FROM **THE WORLD OF RECRUITMENT**

236-243
MEET THE CEO - **GALLERY**

244-245
MORE COMMENTS FROM **THE WORLD OF RECRUITMENT**

LESSONS FROM
THE LEADERS

t is to be recalled that this book was written to address the *why* questions rather than the *how* questions. We hope we may have answered the 'why recruitment?' question, not just via the impressive stats relating to the sector (chapter 2) but by the lived experience of the leaders in this book who have faced the challenges that anyone will need to overcome if they want to follow in their footsteps.

The *how* of recruitment in the sense of the vitally important mechanics of finding clients, candidates and knowing your market and being able to deliver superior value is something that all our leaders' stories touch upon. The *mechanics* or tools of recruitment change always (new technology, new databases, new ways to reach clients and candidates) and at ever greater speed.

But the *principles* and values that underpin success in recruitment (and perhaps business generally) are always relevant and as world renowned success coach Anthony Robbins always says, 'success leaves clues'.

In this chapter we will summarise the clues left by our disparate group of successful leaders. This is much more than a checklist. It is a set of guiding lights if you wish, for when you face the inevitable periods of fog and darkness that will come your way if you wish to emulate these leaders' success.

Another point to bear in mind is that the *way* the leaders have used these principles to lead is always a unique reflection of their individual genius. In other words there is no one 'best' way or model of leadership. This is confirmed in the research conducted by business school scholars. Professor Michael Roberto's work on 'transformational' leadership brilliantly explains that scholars now adhere to a model of 'situational leadership'; different styles of leadership vary in their effectiveness depending on the context.

Returning to the 'secrets' of our featured leaders' success in recruitment the first five principles have been covered in the previous section of the book and they are worth listing again and committing to memory.

Vision
Know where you want to go and define it clearly.
Create a unique mix of value to be different from the competition.

Intuition
Planning is great but expect the unexpected.
Use experience to react rapidly and sustain your competitive advantage.

Courage
Never wait for perfect conditions before following up your flashes of brilliance.
Take the plunge and learn along the way. You will never have all the answers day one.

Fortitude
Setbacks are inevitable.
External conditions will transform economic life but your vision can help you adapt.

Imagination
Don't imitate. Innovate. Best practice is inferior to invention.
The constant flux of the economy creates new opportunities in all sectors.

In addition, there are five other principles that we consider critical and which are embedded in all the stories that we have outlined.

The Ethic of Hard Work
▲ This runs through all the stories and there are no short cuts.
▲ Sue Cooper and Michelle Watson highlight the long hours demanded of them during their successful careers at Michael Page
▲ Dean Kelly as ever in his inimitable 'straight between the eyes' way stresses 'hard work beats talent every time'.

The Power of Influence
▲ All these leaders learnt, mostly through trial and error, the art and science of influence and being able to communicate effectively.
▲ Toni Cocozza was able to strike a deal (when setting up without any capital) to pay her office rent from revenue from the first few deals she secured.
▲ Adam Buck was able to persuade SThree to set up Orgtel to tap into the potential of the telecoms market.
▲ Jason Stewart sought out the investors behind DRC Locums and persuaded them that he knew how to take that business to the next level. He was hired on the spot.

▲ Rob Thesiger persuaded others to back him in his plan to create a new recruitment business specialising in the financial services sector amidst the global financial crisis in 2009!

▲ The central importance and understanding of the ability to influence others is now backed by the latest scholarship in business and psychology. For those interested I refer you to the bestselling *Influence: The Psychology of Persuasion* by Professor Robert Cialdini.

▲ Alternatively try to have coffee with any of the leaders in this book to see the power of persuasion at work!

Embracing Change

▲ Fortitude as we saw above helps to meet the macro changes that are taking place in the globalised economy.

▲ To meet the challenge of these changes and keep ahead of the competition, change has to be an article of faith within any company.

▲ Making that happen is difficult and requires great leadership and making tough choices.

▲ Stuart Britton's example is instructive within the life sciences recruitment space. Despite good growth he took the step to evaluate the whole business to drive a change programme. It ultimately meant taking hard decisions to ensure the right people were at the helm throughout the business.

▲ Adam Shulman had to direct change when the business had reached a point where the benefits of having an external investor were outweighed by the strategic priorities of the business.

Values and People

▲ Recruitment is quintessentially a people business. They are your principal asset in terms of your employees and the source of your service in the form of candidates. And notwithstanding the growth of RPO and other 'intermediary' arrangements, recruitment requires enriching relationships with hirers.

▲ For sustainable and long lasting success, as our leaders in the book so aptly demonstrate, you truly need to value people. And mean it.

▲ That will be the secret ingredient to building great teams and a culture that is the bedrock of any brand or business.

▲ As Darren Ryemill says: *"culture eats strategy for breakfast"* and that is why he seeks to encourage ambition and drive and the hunger associated with a start-up even to this day.

▲ Toni Cocozza and Karen Silk have deeply loyal teams with tremendous records of longevity of service because their values drive their businesses.

▲ Numerous others have senior leaders within their organisations who began as trainee recruiters (Adam Buck, Sue Cooper to name two) and John Hailstone created a model for his senior leaders to give them a stake in the future of the business.

▲ Greg Latham, learning from his own bitter experience, ensured from inception that his business offered every employee a 'John Lewis' type participation.

▲ Stuart Britton personally runs a values workshop for everyone who joins the business.

Self-development

▲ All our leaders have demonstrated a lifelong desire for self-improvement.

▲ Many were, by their own admission, drifting along in careers where they felt something was missing but wanted to realise their potential.

▲ Some undertook formal training to improve their understanding of business such as Andy Hogarth training to be an accountant and David Cook attending courses at Cranfield.

▲ All have striven to master the intricacies of an ever more complex world of business and had the self-belief that they could do so.

▲ It's a mindset of a winning leader: to find a way to master the next phase of their journey.

THE FUTURE OF RECRUITMENT
IS HERE NOW

The principles outlined in the previous chapter and personified by each of our leaders in this book will be tested ever more powerfully as the world of work and the recruitment sector moves further into the 21st century.

In the words of leading digital, social and mobile strategist within the recruitment sector, Matt Adler: *"Technology is redefining the labour market at lightning speed and this disruption is only going to get bigger and move faster in the next few years."*

At the CIETT World Employment Conference 2016 held in New Delhi, the message was even more pointed: *"The future of work is here"* was the overriding message. Annemarie Muntz, CIETT President, highlighted that:

"The world of work is changing. The labour market is facing a series of challenges such as digitisation, globalisation,

TECHNOLOGY IS REDEFINING THE LABOUR MARKET AT LIGHTNING SPEED AND THIS DISRUPTION IS ONLY GOING TO GET BIGGER AND MOVE FASTER IN THE NEXT FEW YEARS.

demographic change, skills shortages and new attitudes to work."

In this chapter we touch upon a few of the trends that are challenging the current recruitment model and outline some of the advice offered by our leaders.

Growth of In-House Recruitment

Particularly in light of the pressure on profit margins experienced by the economy following the recent global financial crisis (together with the ubiquity of online platforms such as LinkedIn - more on this below), there has been evidence of hirers across the private and public sectors investing in growing their in-house recruitment capability to reduce reliance on agencies.

Our leaders have responded to this trend in a number of ways which offer valuable tools moving forward. John Hailstone at Compello Group specifically re-configured his business model to offer more specialist services in order to counter this threat.

Others such as Karen Silk at Capital International Staffing and Richard Herring at Volt highlight the importance of strengthening relationships with clients and adding value in respect of the search for senior talent as creative ways to accommodate this trend.

Globalisation and International Talent Pools

The mega trend of globalisation of the last couple of decades has lifted millions out of poverty and seen the omnipresence of the Chinese economy across the value chain in manifold industries. Consumers in the developed world have benefited from cheaper manufactured goods and global trade has increased as the world economy has become more integrated. The expansion of the EU has offered access to talent across many sectors for the UK economy with perhaps healthcare, construction and hospitality being the most prominent beneficiaries.

Looking ahead following the Brexit, vote recruiters will now need to call upon all their skills as advocates of the benefits of a flexible and open labour market as the UK economy enters into a period of prolonged economic uncertainty.

Indeed, recruiters now categorically have an imperative to make this case as the Government begins the search for talent to help with Brexit-related trade negotiations, so an opportunity to make margin and help the nation. Recruitment offers it all!

Speaking on the day after the Referendum Kevin Greene, the CEO at the REC, was strident that in the aftermath of the Leave vote:

"Access to talent is absolutely vital to sustainable economic growth and prosperity. In sectors such as healthcare, education, hospitality, construction and manufacturing workers from the EU are vital and any change to our immigration system needs to recognise that."

FUNDAMENTALLY WE ARE STILL A PEOPLE INDUSTRY AND WE ARE STILL AS STRONG AS EVER AS A PROFESSION. PEOPLE NEED PEOPLE, NOT ALGORITHMS TO HELP THEM MAKE CRUCIAL DECISIONS IN THEIR LIFE."

Policy makers should be required to read Albert Ellis' moving and powerful comments about the importance of having an open labour market.

Technology and Digital Platforms

Job Boards followed by Social media platforms (LinkedIn in particular) have become an all pervading presence within the world of recruitment. Both were seen as existential threats by some within recruitment but the reality has been different.

In terms of LinkedIn Steve Ingham CEO at Page Group has eloquently argued that it *"...remains a channel, not a true alternative. In a world where the competition amongst employers for high quality talent is fiercer than ever, the need for expert professional recruitment partners is critical."*

Another much vaunted transformation offered by technology is the rise of 'workforce intermediation platforms' which directly match workers with engagers whether for an entire project or discrete elements within it. Upwork, TaskRabbit and Uber are differentiated manifestations of the so-called 'gig' economy. Whilst celebrated economist Tim Harford, (writing in December 2015), has said that *"the app-based gig economy is still small,"* the fact that in 2014 Uber had 160,000 active drivers in the US and delivered more than $650 million in payments in the forth quarter of that year has made people and the recruitment sector sit up and take notice.

The potential benefits for the global economy of such gig platforms has been recognised. McKinsey Global Institute in its June 2015 Report contends that some 850 million working age people globally are 'under-utilised' (either unemployed, inactive or working only part time) and that by 2025 *"..online talent platforms could raise global GDP by $2.7 trillion and increase employment by 72 million full-time equivalent positions."*

Without even delving into the potential disruption that robotics may cause to labour markets it is clear that recruiters face profound questions from technological change and the 'online talent platforms' described by McKinsey.

Our leaders, whilst recognising the lightning pace of technological change impacting the labour market, caution against being overwhelmed. Instead they counsel recourse to the essence of recruitment: people.

"I remember some saying job boards and then LinkedIn were going to replace recruiters. They didn't and in fact recruiters are now lead users of these tools within their businesses. I see the same with the online talent platforms which may in any event not operate in the highly skilled core markets of professional recruiters. In fact, if they help more people into the world of work that means opportunity for recruiters!" says Darren Ryemill.

Perhaps the last word can be left to Sue Cooper who began her recruitment career in 1980:

"Fundamentally we are still a people industry and we are still as strong as ever as a profession. People need people, not algorithms to help them make crucial decisions in their life."

"I REMEMBER SOME SAYING JOB BOARDS AND THEN LINKEDIN WERE GOING TO REPLACE RECRUITERS. THEY DIDN'T AND IN FACT RECRUITERS ARE NOW LEAD USERS OF THESE TOOLS WITHIN THEIR BUSINESSES.

FINAL THOUGHT
THE MEDIUM
IS THE MESSAGE

*"Setting an example is not the main means of influencing others
...it is the only means."*
- Albert Einstein (attributed)

It has been a privilege to share the stories of the leaders in this book. It has been a privilege to get to know the leaders and with some develop sincere and enriching friendships over the years.

It is my hope as said at the outset that the stories act as sources of inspiration for those working in the recruitment sector either new to it or long established. That it is possible to reach the pinnacle within the sector wherever you may currently be in your career.

The stories are also designed to counter the often unjustified criticisms levelled at recruitment and to repair the tarnished reputation that haunts it, despite the great work undertaken in the past decade to raise standards.

Chapter 9 sought to capture the 'secrets' (or perennial principles) that underpin the uplifting accomplishments of the leaders featured in this book. In our broader popular culture which is saturated with symbols of the quick fix, where quantity reigns over quality and activity is mistaken for accomplishment, the ethics, hard work and determination (often over many years) demonstrated in the journeys of these leaders acts as a welcome corrective; that there are no short cuts and business and life demand a fair price from those seeking the substantial rewards on offer.

But perhaps even the list set out in chapter 9 does not give the entire message that the stories contain. For one central element runs through every one of these stories and encompasses all the 'secrets of success'. And that is the medium through which these leaders have been able to create such legacies of success and inspiration.

That medium is the nature of the recruitment sector itself. Perhaps its unique characteristics as an industry constitute the most powerful message of this collection of stories.

It is accepted that the sector like all others is far from perfect. There are those that take a principled stance arguing that it should be more regulated to create barriers to entry and making it harder for people to enter it. This is an argument worth debating but it must not be forgotten that highly regulated sectors such as accountancy and the world of banking proved no guarantee against unscrupulous behaviour with damaging economic consequences that engulfed the whole of society; think Enron and the Global Financial Crisis's creation of ever more exotic financial instruments (anyone fancy a synthetic CDO?)

So perhaps for all its imperfections it is the recruitment sector itself that should stand as the one overarching 'secret' to be applauded.

For if there is one message from these stories for those seeking to be rewarded in accordance with the value they add, it is surely this:

Whoever you are, whatever your background, whatever your age, your qualifications (or lack thereof) and whatever your current situation if you have a desire to succeed, are willing to work hard and are truly motivated to help people then we in recruitment open our doors to you. You can author your own story, you are welcome and there are many who have shown the way and would help you to achieve your dreams.

It may be argued that the leaders featured in this book had the traits within them that would have guaranteed their success in any industry. One can see the force of that argument and indeed many had successful previous careers before entering *"the wonderful world of recruitment"* as Joost Kreulen describes the sector.

But it is important to remember just how far our leaders have come in many cases: if one had met an Andy Hogarth or Richard Herring in the immediate years after they left education (both confess to hardly being trailblazers career-wise during those periods) or Toni Cocozza as she left school without any qualifications (and being severely dyslexic), could one have guessed where they would reach in their careers via the recruitment industry? One could conduct similar thought experiments for many of the others in this book.

It is, in my view, the unique nature of the recruitment sector itself that shines through as the very special context that permitted our featured leaders to realise their potential. That has not changed. Wherever you may be in your career or working life today is not where you need remain; to repeat, the recruitment sector is a powerful meritocracy open to all. Long may it remain so.

I leave with the words of Richard Herring which remain as apposite today as they have ever been:

"This business is fundamentally predicated on understanding the needs of people. So, provided you do your job properly and always strive to add value to your clients and candidates you will thrive. It is a fantastic career choice."

"THIS BUSINESS IS FUNDAMENTALLY PREDICATED ON UNDERSTANDING THE NEEDS OF PEOPLE.

BIBLIOGRAPHY
AND REFERENCES

23 Things They Don't Tell You About Capitalism
Chang, Ha-Joon
Penguin Books   2011

Influence: The Psychology of Persuasion
Cialdini, Robert B.
Harper Collins   2007

On War
Clausewitz, Carl Von
Wordsworth Editions   1997

Good to Great
Collins, Jim
Random House   2001

Only the Paranoid Survive
Grove, Andrew S.
Harper Collins   1997

The Luck Factor
Gunther, Max
Macmillan Publishing   1977

Made to Stick
Heath, Chip and Dan
Arrow Books   2008

Building the Best Jobs Market in the World
REC   2015

Blue Ocean Strategy
Kim, W. Chan and Renée Mauborgne
Harvard Business Review Press   2015

The Power of Intuition:
How to Use Your Gut Feelings to Make Better Decisions at Work
Klein, Gary A.
Crown Business   2004

What Management Is
Magretta, Joan
Profile Books   2003

Understanding Michael Porter
Magretta, Joan
Harvard Business Review Press   2012

Different: Escaping the Competitive Herd
Moon, Youngme
Crown Business   2010

What is Strategy?
Porter, Michael
Harvard Business Review   1996

Competitive Strategy
Porter, Michael E
New York: Free Press   1980

The Lean Startup
Ries, Eric
Portfolio Penguin   2011

Good Strategy, Bad Strategy
Rumelt, Richard
Profile Books   2011

The Global Gender Gap Report
World Economic Forum   2014

A Labour Market that Works
McKinsey Global Institute   2015

COMMENTS FROM **THE RECRUITMENT WORLD**

"Suhail's writing is both insightful and compelling and is well regarded in the Recruitment industry."

Paul Jameson
Founder and CEO - Outsource UK

"Suhail demonstrates a thorough knowledge of current issues of political economy and how these affect the dynamics in the staffing industry. He has the capability to write lucidly on often complex issues and I look forward to reading more from him."

Joost Kreulen
CEO - Empresaria Group plc

"Suhail and I have collaborated on a number of initiatives, he is very knowledgeable and well networked in the recruitment sector, and a consummate professional, this guy has his ear to the ground!"

Nick Stevens
Co-Founder - Eximius Group & Director - Capital Selection

"Suhail is very well connected within the recruitment industry and is a good person to do business with."

Andrew Pettingill
Managing Director - Meridien Business Support

"Suhail is an incredibly well connected individual and a fountain of knowledge on a lot of different matters. One of a kind."

James Ballard
Co-Founder - Annapurna HR

"I have been impressed by Suhail particularly with what I consider to be an ethical approach to his journalistic work. His wide experience of business – he has owned, managed and recently sold his enterprise - is evident. I admire and enjoy Suhail's coverage of the recruitment sector."

Craig Vidler
Managing Director - Prima Pincipia

"Suhail's knowledge of the recruitment sector is excellent and his network is impressive. I have been particularly impressed with his writing skills and thoroughly enjoy reading his various articles."

Andrea Williams
Managing Director - Ambition

MEET THE CEO
GALLERY

DEAN KELLY
CEO - SYNARBOR PLC

ROBERT THESIGER
CEO - FISER GROUP

JANE LOVELL
MANAGING DIRECTOR
COOPER LOMAZ

ALAN MCBRIDE
MANAGING DIRECTOR
CAMINO PARTNERS

JULIE O'NEILL
MANAGING DIRECTOR
MCCALL

DARREN RYEMILL
CEO - OPUS PROFESSIONAL
SERVICES GROUP

SUE COOPER
CEO - MORGAN HUNT

SCOTT BULLOCH
MANAGING DIRECTOR
ATA RECRUITMENT

MIKE GAWTHORNE
CEO - SEROCOR GROUP

STUART BRITTON
CEO - RDL
CORPORATION

PAUL JAMESON
MANAGING DIRECTOR
OUTSOURCE UK

GREG LATHAM
MANAGING DIRECTOR
ENCORE PERSONNEL

PAM EASEN
CEO - H1 HEALTHCARE

TONI COCOZZA
MANAGING DIRECTOR
DP CONNECT

CHARLIE WALKER
FORMER CEO
VIVID RESOURCING

ADAM SHULMAN
CEO - SIMPLY EDUCATION

DAVID COOK
MANAGING DIRECTOR
NATIONAL LOCUMS

MATTHEW EAMES
CEO - EAMES CONSULTING

ANDY HOGARTH
CEO - STAFFLINE

ALBERT ELLIS
CEO - HARVEY NASH

RICHARD HERRING
MANAGING DIRECTOR
VOLT

MICHELLE WATSON
CEO - GEMINI PEOPLE

JOHN HAILSTONE
CEO - COMPELLO
STAFFING GROUP

KAREN SILK
CEO - CAPITAL
INTERNATIONAL STAFFING

JASON STEWART
CEO - DRC LOCUMS

STEVE INGHAM
CEO - PAGEGROUP

GARY ASHWORTH
CHAIRMAN - INTERQUEST
GROUP PLC

ADAM BUCK
CEO - PHAIDON
INTERNATIONAL

ANDREA WILLIAMS
MANAGING DIRECTOR
AMBITION

DAVID RAI
CEO - TESTING CIRCLE

ANDREW LARHOLT
CEO - MONTASH

JOOST KREULEN
CEO - EMPRESARIA
GROUP PLC

MORE COMMENTS FROM **THE RECRUITMENT WORLD**

"I have had business dealings with Suhail over the past 10 years during my time as CEO of staffing businesses. He is well connected in recruitment and his City Page column also demonstrates his understanding of the recruitment space."

Ross Eades
CEO - Horton International
Former CEO - Interquest Group plc

"Having a conversation with Suhail always results in a great learning experience, thanks to the depth of his knowledge on a wide range of topics. His views are always interesting and thought provoking. Most of all, I value Suhail's integrity tremendously, which certainly stands out in our industry."

Greet Brosens
Group Sales & Marketing Director - Adecco Group

"Suhail has done a great job of researching and understanding the recruitment marketplace."

Ian Temple
CEO - Hydrogen Group

"Suhail is the go-to person in our sector for up-to-date City information in the recruitment sector - his incisive comments are very well judged and informative."

Dave Pye
Former CEO - JM Group

"Suhail is a well-connected, respected and informed member of the recruitment and wider business community. He is a pleasure to talk to and offers valuable insight and opinion that has proved very useful as I grow my business in a competitive industry."

Andrew Larholt
CEO - Montash

"Suhail's understanding, experience and wide people network means he has valuable insights for recruitment entrepreneurs."

Steve Wright
CEO - ReThink Group

MEET THE CEO
JOURNEY TO THE TOP

Published 2016

Designed by RACS Marketing Limited
www.racsmarketing.com

Illustrations: Josh Trim

Designers: Zoe Tabourajis
                Sandra Morgan
                Jon Sheahan

Proofing: Ann Hanlon

Supported by:
Recruitment International   RACS Group

"Whoever you are, whatever your background, whatever your age, your qualifications (or lack thereof) and whatever your current situation if you have a desire to succeed, are you willing to work hard and are truly motivated to help people then we in recruitment open our doors to you. You can author your own story, you are welcome and there are many who have shown the way and would help you achieve your dreams."